SHEENA PATEL is a writer and assistant director for the film and TV industry. She has previously published *This Is What Love is*, a pamphlet with 4 BROWN GIRLS WHO WRITE (Rough Trade Books, 2020), and she was named as one of the *Observer*'s Top Ten debut novelists for *I'm a Fan*.

'Mining the darkest depths of coercion, seduction and abuser dynamics ... This is a novel centred around voice, and Patel's is unique and powerful' *Observer*

'Written in brief, aphoristic segments, like mini-blogs or Instagram posts, it charts the moods and frustrations of an unnamed young woman in thrall to a toxic older lover' *Financial Times*

'Surely you have found your perfect summer read. Sheena Patel's debut novel is that very book ... Patel has called *I'm a Fan* "an imagined act of revenge verging on performance art". If that sounds a bit intense, that's because it is. Bring on the beach breakdowns!' *Independent*

'Patel brings immediacy and pace to her story ... And despite her problematic actions, the novel's central character is deeply likeable' *New Statesman*

I'M A FAN

SHEENA PATEL

GRANTA

Granta Publications, 12 Addison Avenue, London W11 4QR

First published in hardback in Great Britain by Rough Trade Books in 2022

This paperback edition published by Granta Books in 2023

A CIP catalogue record for this book is available from the British Library.

10 9 8 7 6 5 4 3

ISBN 978 1 78378 981 8
eISBN 978 1 78378 982 5

Offset by Patty Rennie
Printed and bound by CPI Group (UK) Ltd, Croydon, CR0 4YY

www.granta.com

I stalk a woman on the internet who is sleeping with the same man as I am. Sometimes when I am too quick to look at her stories, I block her temporarily so she doesn't know I absent-mindedly refresh her page fifteen times a minute while Netflix plays in the background on my laptop, my stomach flipping sick with delight when her profile picture is ringed red. She has tens of thousands of followers, is verified, and is the daughter of someone famous in America. An endless stream of white people fawn in the comments under her posts. She has opinions about household objects which I have never given a thought to before; firm taste in the types of beeswax candles to burn, lays exquisite cloth on her table in anticipation of dinner, knows where to buy limited edition pottery from well-regarded potters, she will happily spend $300 on a vase where she displays really, really organic fennel flowers, by which she says there is organic and then *organic*, buys a $500 ring for herself during a time of financial strife for the rest of the world and shows it off in a selfie. She uses a filter on Instagram which burns up her flaws, it thins down her cheeks and radioactively erases the two thick lines shaped like spooning 'v's which are carved in her forehead and erupt from her face more prominently when she raises her eyebrows. A sick sense of satisfaction rips through me when I see them. She orders take-out from the right restaurants, seems to know everyone in the higher echelons of society, is accepted into the kind of circles which seem out of reach to me. Sometimes I wonder if I ever met her, what would I say to her, would I tell her of our connection? Would I tell her I know where she lives, would I tell her how I guessed that she broke up with her boyfriend. Will I tell her I know why the tone of her stories changed because the man we are both sleeping with, the man I want to be with, shamed her for exploiting her privacy the last time they saw one another. Would I tell her that I know who her ex-husband is, I've seen his new family and he seems happy now, happier than the photos I've seen of the two of them, would I tell her I know who all her friends are and I watch their stories too, would I tell her I screenshot the photos she takes of herself and study her face so intently sometimes I fear I've picked up some facial expressions or tonal inflections from her because I listen to her speaking with her father on YouTube over and over before I go to sleep. Would I move in closer to smell her and feel what he felt when he felt her—*would I taste the inside of your mouth to find out what was so compelling, would I press into you, I want to know exactly how your body moves when you are turned on—to know for myself why he cancelled fucking me to fuck you.*

tell me what i want

I refresh, refresh, refresh, refresh. The woman I am obsessed with usually posts around this time. I'm half-watching *Gilmore Girls* on my laptop. I refresh again and suddenly on the ninth refresh, the squares shuffle to the right, go white, quickly blink back into colour and there's a new post—a selection of the products she sells from a web-shop she owns called Terroir. It may or may not make a profit but regardless of this minor inconvenience, it seems that being a founder of an independent web-shop is the new rich kid thing to do. All her friends have variations of this curated online presence where they push a skincare line or expensive household furniture, or cookware—objects which have been taken outside of their cultural contexts to be placed artfully in your home to make you appear more interesting. I've learnt about mid-century furniture this way. I think of my parents' generic in-built wardrobes in fake wood that I'm sure is veneered plastic which they proudly picked out of the company magazine from a wholesaler warehouse in Sudbury.

I know the woman I am obsessed with has many of these tastemaker friends, where the acquisition of beauty seems to fuel them as much as food. One of these friends posts notable artists' interiors like she does. I know this as I stalk him too in case he posts photos of her because I like to know what she wears every day, which makes me feel shit but then makes me feel like I've achieved something when I know but really, I lose a tiny part of myself every time I screenshot a photo of her or her new studio flat in Marfa now she's single or her previous flat she shared with her ex-boyfriend or her father's house where I try to map the geography of the rooms. I save these screenshots to the Album in my phone which, when I scroll through, looks deceptively like I have

3

a very good friend whose life I celebrate, as if I want to treasure her memories alongside my own. I don't have any opinions about furniture. If I was to ever have a home I'm not sure what I would fill it with. I don't own anything that would tell other people how much of a tastemaker I am, how much of a grown-up. I fit into spaces which already exist and contort myself to fit a shape which has been allocated for me. I don't own anything. The thought of antique shopping for each individual item is exhausting and exhilarating and expensive. I click through to the shops the woman I am obsessed with tags in her posts, who she thanks, the painters she recommends on her stories, helpfully including a link to buy one for yourself. I look up the price of a painting she angles into the sun, on top of her brightly coloured mantlepiece with the hashtags of the architect who built it and the painter who painted the painting. I google the artist's name and 'price' and he's dead and his work costs between fifteen and twenty thousand dollars and my jaw swings open and I want to own it too but how and where do you go to buy paintings? Or perhaps what I want is the disposable cash to be able to buy a painting but actually what I want is something much harder to attain which is to know what paintings are worth buying in the first place combined with the innate belief I deserve to be in surroundings that need paintings on the walls before I am able to feel at home. I read the caption on the new post and it says, *meet us at our pop-up at a friend's house in Notting Hill, dm for details*. The post is a graphic amalgamation of the items Terroir sells, the objects hung disembodied on a white background. The uniqueness of her business is that she is a daughter of someone who is famous for being aesthetically rigorous and if you part with a minimum of $500 you might be able to buy into this upbringing too. I think—this is my chance.

I check the address and Maps guides me past the high-rises to a leafy street ten minutes' walk from Notting Hill Gate station. It's the kind of street where there are no 'for sale' signs because everyone here knows they have a good thing, the kind of street where each door is painted the same tone of a different colour, to tell you—*there's community here, we talk to our neighbours and think about things like the aesthetics of front doors*. Their front doors are not the white plastic doors which I've been brought up looking at—the ones which replicate like a DNA sequence right through Kingsbury, where passing the first threshold you are led to a small, intermediate space to kick off your shoes before passing another white plastic door which brings you into the bulk of the house. These doors are bespoke doors, grand-looking one-offs from antique fairs or else original features which come with the listed house, painted in poetically branded Farrow & Ball colours. There aren't just red and white and brilliant white, they don't have names like 'brave beige' and 'mermaid sheen', no, these colours announce themselves like a discreet sommelier at a nice restaurant who murmurs *excellent choice*. Here, beige is split into *bone, pigeon, tallow, wevet*—beige is not beige in this kind of taste-country, it is rustically referenced to make you believe you are cleverer than you are and you deserve to be gently handled.

I walk over to a particularly lovely house, off-set from the pavement by an ornately patterned tiled drive with a crescent shaped rose bush that affords a semblance of privacy to the large bay windows. It is an indulgent and imposing family home that swishes its generational wealth-tail. There is jewelled stained glass above a wide door that is footed by three steps in a half moon.

A clapped-out Citroën in the drive only serves to amplify the river of money that I sense cascades over the house. I hold the doorknob in my hand. It is brass and reassuringly heavy. I breathe deeply. Am I really about to do this? I've decided to wear the closest things to designer brands that I own but to look slightly edgy, I cap my outfit with gleaming white Nike Air Force Ones that I baby wipe after each use to keep them box fresh, second-hand Ganni tracksuit bottoms, a Stüssy sports bra with a crumpled, second hand designer shirt that I button once at the centre revealing my doughy middle. I throw a glance at the Citroën. I wonder if my crumpled is the same as a rich person's crumpled. I hold the brass knocker in my hand.

dick from someone who doesn't care if you live or die

The man I want to be with is play-fighting with me in the park. He pushes my head down into the grass, sits on my back and tickles me. I wriggle out from under him, throw him off and stand crouched, my hands out in front of me, my fingers spread in the air like ten worms emerging from the earth. I trap him in a headlock. He tickles me again and trips me, guiding me down to the ground. When I stand up, I am so overexcited I drool and saliva globs out from my mouth and it shines on the back of my hand. I am suddenly aware of the parameters of my body slammed against his body. This is the most physical contact he allows. He says the sex is too intense between us which is why we don't do it anymore. He has a beautiful cock—straight and thick and very long. When he used to let me fuck him, he would be so deep inside me I could map the edges of my cervix, I had to ask him to go very slow as my eyes rolled back to moan. Even the memory of it makes my knickers sticky and I've just accidentally-on-purpose brushed my hand against his trousers to check if he's hard and he is. He's hard but he won't fuck me and I'm so turned on I know I will have to resort to going through our very old emails to unearth his unsolicited dick pics and wank to those when I am home.

I ask him if he's heard from the woman I am obsessed with and he says no. I say, her book has come out, she's doing tons of interviews. He says, I know, someone I'm friends with in America sent me a link to one of them and it's cringe, I can't bear to look at it. I don't tell him how I've been monitoring her book release like I'm planning a drone strike. Over time, I've learnt I need to ask very specific questions because the truth fractures in his mouth. He tells me a version by omission, which puts the responsibility onto me to ask the right questions in just the right way, almost as if I am a lawyer grilling a witness in court. However, he will often disarm me by giving me too much information and so if I am hurt, he says, well it's because you asked, and if I find out later that something was different to how he told me it is, he says, well you didn't ask the right question. He says, she received a $350,000 advance for her book, and I gasp and my hand flies to my mouth, and he says, she'll get an extra $50,000 if it hits the bestseller list, and I gape, I ask, has she hit it, and he says, I don't know, so we google it and scan through the previous lists but we can't find it anywhere. Soon enough, he is distracted. I watch his fingers automatically check his email, his Instagram, his WhatsApp, back to his email again, his Instagram, the news. I look at him absorbed inside his phone. To regain his attention, I pounce on him and push him down so his back is flat against the grass and I sit on top of him, his phone tumbling out of his hand. I place the centre of my cunt on the bottom of his cock. It's so nice sitting on the heft of him even through our clothes, but he won't let me have him naked I know this. I start by laughing, like, look at me, oh I'm so light-hearted and fun and kaa-ray-zee! I pin his arms back over his head and I laugh because this is a light-hearted jovial waterboarding. I ask him if he's going to be with me. He tries to throw me off with his legs but I clamp down to secure myself. Are you going to be with me? I repeat, say yes or no. I laugh so he knows this could be a joke. He laughs back nervously but is wriggling from under me. I sense my creeping desperation—say yes or no, the words brittle through my gritted teeth. I put more weight into my hands, we're still having fun, this is still fun isn't it. He screws up his face and says, you're hurting my hands. My head lowers down in front of his and I snarl, I want you to say no for fuck's sake, I want you to tell me no. He throws me off because he is stronger than me, panting with the effort because I am bigger than him. We glare at one another. I have to go home, he says as he looks towards the sky now stained orange and pink. He looks back at me and says, it's getting late. My chest is creaking. I silently start to pack the picnic I brought back into my bag looking down trying to think of a last-ditch way to turn this around in my favour and force him to profess his undying love for me and give me the promise I need which is his hand in marriage. I know he has to leave because he has to be home with his wife before dinner. We rise and I pick the blanket up which I laid down for us, to show him I can leave him quite abruptly, I am not clingy, here I am able to leave him.

He stands in front of me. I want to hurt him. Are we building to a future? I ask. He is petrified as if suddenly aware of a predator. I press on: are you using our meet-ups as fact-finding missions to make a decision or is this enough for you? I abandon the folding of the blanket into nice, neat edges and hold it chaotically in my arms. He becomes very focused as he tips dregs of tea out of my flask, spots his phone on the ground and slips it back into his pocket. He keeps his head down and says, I can't answer that question in that way, I can see a future with you but it's too specific a question. A buzzing erupts in my ears. I beat the grass off the blanket to drown out the sound. Sometimes I wonder are you the main relationship in my life, he says tipping his head up to absorb the weakening sun. I narrow my eyes and curl my lips in disdain, and I say, of course I'm the main relationship in your life. The man I want to be with walks towards me. He reaches his hand out to take some grass out of my hair but I smack him off me and push his shoulder sharply to jerk him back. He rocks on his heels, tries to regain his balance. I focus on a tiny tree in the distance to steady me.

If I stare hard enough maybe I can disappear it. I sense a tingling in my abdomen, like teeth sprouting out of gums in my stomach, little headstones marking out every injury.

The glob of saliva starts to crust on my hand in the sun.

The man I want to be with does not offer up his number at the beginning and so I do not ask. He emails which is clunky and cumbersome but there is an unspoken understanding he does not want to be easily contactable by me. We have short bursts of intense contact which I increasingly have to initiate and then nothing for weeks in between. He is in Hydra in Greece installing a joint show of work with his wife. I'm not supposed to know about this show but I do (cos Instagram), and in our scant messages, I pretend I don't know who he is with or where, because upon his return this coming weekend we will be meeting again. I am at work in a darkened studio when I see his name flash on my phone, I open the email eagerly but as I scan the words I start to lose my balance. He tells me he won't be able to make the dick appointment he's made with me, a recent ex has asked to see him and the only time he is available is when we have arranged to meet. He writes, it is quite inconvenient she wants to see him as currently he and his wife are getting along quite well however, it is torturous between him and this woman, the physical relationship is addictive and heady. They have started talking again and I realise this is why it has been particularly hard to hold his attention lately. He tells me he's not sure he'd be up for having sex with me if he sees me afterwards so it's best to cancel our meeting. It seems he cannot let go of her—you can't get rid of love, he says wetly. The email is a confession, an unburdening from him to me. He tells me they ran into each other a couple of months ago at a private view at the Royal Academy but he was so distressed he walked out. She texted him and asked him why he left and he replied, it was too much for him to see her. I realise many things very quickly. She is better in bed than me. She has his number which means he wants to be easily contactable by her. I am not embarking on the start of a love affair which gets me out of my relationship and into one with him where my real life can begin. Even though he is cheating on his wife and I am cheating on my boyfriend and that means neither of us is trustworthy, he is already in love with someone outside of this equilibrium of entanglements and feels no loyalty to me, which then also reveals I expect special treatment from him of some kind, a selflessness no one in this web is giving anyone else. She is more important to him than I am, and I have made no real impression on him. There is a whole other storyline unfolding with two main characters and I am merely the short subplot to aid the trajectory of their love story. I am not a main character in this ensemble romcom of betrayal, I am a supporting act. He is in no danger of falling in love with me. I am usurpable in my own life. I am on a lower social stratum to the two of them and in this way they are equals and are better matched. No one would think to invite me to a private view at the Royal Academy—I am no one. I'm a fan and because of this, I can be cut out.

window shopping

I recognise the woman who opens the door from Instagram.
Her name is Val. She has an older boyfriend, possibly husband, but I can't
be sure from my research. She was brought up in Mendocino too and
I know she works part-time for Terroir but rather than a job to survive,
it's a hobby—it's like a nice thing to do. Val takes pictures of herself in
the mirror using her iPhone to block her face, or close-ups of beautiful
fabrics, or a single photo of an exhibition she's gone to and tags the
artist with a personalised message because she is friends with them. She
declares her love for her boyfriend/husband often. As a couple they
favour the lift selfie and she posts these in her stories. She takes photos
of objects wrapped in delicate fabrics edged with lace fronds or else with
acid-coloured string around exquisite brown paper and posts these to
her grid. Under these posts, she is rewarded with comments of fluttering
hearts and hands-up emojis from her friends. The woman I am obsessed
with comments 'gorgeous'—a trademark of hers is to write one-word
comments under her friends' posts.

Val is glossy but pared down. She is dressed plainly but her
clothes are cut sharply at the shoulder and the waist which makes her
appear more beautiful, or more intimidating which I suppose is the same
thing. Her shoes are tan leather with a ball on the heel like a building
block. It's so her, so her taste, kooky and timeless. I start to feel uneasy
in my trainers and my crumpled shirt. She asks me what my name is,
she checks it off her iPad, smiles widely and says, follow me, and walks
down a long corridor without checking to see if I'm behind her. There
is more stained glass, the patterns of light flutter across the walls. The
house is dark but up-lit somehow and the furniture is made entirely of

dark, chocolatey wood. The floor has a buckled quality which tells you how old it is by virtue of how dead the wood is like you're in a grand country house. She leads me to the living room. She flattens out her hand to show me where the 'pieces' are and tells me she'll be back in fifteen minutes, I should feel free to try anything on but not the jewellery on display, they have a separate set they can offer if I like the look of anything. She'll let me browse and will check on me. I smile and say thank you. I wander aimlessly around the room. There are huge paintings on the wall with flashes of red and pink, the wallpaper is textured, like a plastering effect before the paint goes on. I touch it. The thinking behind the unfinishedness is connected to owning the Citroën outside. To leave the walls this way is not because of monetary constraint, it is a design choice. There is wealth evident everywhere so there is no need to try so hard. Various objects that have no apparent use but look expensive are dotted about the room—very small dishes and bowls displayed on the mantlepiece in bright colours with nothing in them, there are brass candlesticks with indigo and yellow beeswax candles lit inside them, the type and the kind the woman I am obsessed with prefers. I can see evidence of her everywhere but especially in the overbearing bouquets punctuating the room, intimidating arrays of sweet peas and branches and gaping white flowers. These floral hand-picked concertos arranged by the woman I am obsessed with have a confidence occupying this space in a way I can only aspire to. On a presentation rack, the cream, navy and black outdoor jumpsuits, made in a fashion atelier in Milan, to be worn especially for your Instagrammable gardening but chic enough to wear to your Instagrammable farmer's market (£1k), are hung with large spaces between them. There are gold rings set with pearls (£8k). Next to this on a Paul McCobb cabinet are gardening tools costing between £400 and £800 with a small handwritten label next to them with her logo on the top which says they are made by the practice of *shokunin*—an artisanal philosophy that apparently mirrors her own. On the floor stacked like passengers awaiting the arrival of a train are handmade leather boots shipped in from Italy (£900), handwoven baskets made by white women weavers to replicate the ones she once saw in a market in Oaxaca (£750) to pick vegetables in a photogenic way from your sprawling garden. I have stared at all of these through my phone screen and it's now jarring to look at them in the flesh. The boots are in a butter-like leather, they look so expensive but also look like nothing remarkable but would also demand a certain kind of treatment from other people. Having hovered over these for so long, nine hundred pounds has started to look quite reasonable, why wouldn't you spend nine hundred on shoes, a grand on a jumpsuit—but £1200 (minus bills) per month is the amount of rent I struggle to make with my boyfriend.

    I drift to the dining table which has been moved aside for the presentation. The chairs look vintage but are top of the range design classics, are all interestingly mismatched and because they don't stack are set in a row next to each other. On the table there is a lilac tablecloth commissioned from an artist who has embroidered plant motifs onto the fabric (£350) and there are crudités presented in wooden bowls, but not the kind of dry, neglected crudités I have seen on the tables of most subpar white people events I've attended. This is a different bar, a more confident display of whiteness. These vegetables still retain their wildness from the earth presented with their stalks, the carrots are in juicy rainbow colours—I've never seen purple, red or yellow carrots before—radishes still whole with their leaves attached, mini cucumbers and fennel cut lengthways with assertive edges. There are stacks of rough-hewn loaves of sourdough and rye bread—I wonder if they are decoration—and plaited lengths of baguette threading their way under them, the baker's hands evident in their lovingly patted crusty skins. Bunches of red grapes are voluptuously draped near them on metallic plates. In two white bowls with deep blue edging, there is regular hummus and some red dip which has swooshes dug out of it. I can tell people have been here before me by how much hummus has been eaten and from the small pile of discarded stems in the bowl. On a lime green plate with ceramic fringing lays one of their silk Georgia O'Keefe flower scarves (£600), under the scarf I find a Nancy Silverton limited edition bread knife (£169 but not available as it is sold out). The scene is lit from one of the large windows opposite me, which lends the table this romantic Modern-meets-seventeenth century Dutch still life vibe and I think how the fuck do you know how to do this. And where the fuck are you. There seems to be no one else in the house. I can't afford anything and I don't want to even pretend to try. At that moment I hear Val's footsteps coming through the hallway and I scramble to be seen considering the boots, so it turns out I do want to pretend to try. She pops her head in and her face is set to forbearance, she knows I can't afford anything, her smile is politely wan. I'm not one of her people. I say, maybe not today, I'll order through Terroir if I change my mind and her smile becomes thinner and she says, of course, you know where to find us. She steps back to walk me to the front door, her mouth stretched to a straight line. I check Terroir's socials later and the woman I am obsessed with screeches in a post, *thanks to all who came we were so happy to meet you, thank you for supporting a small business*. The text is laid over a photo of one of their billowing scarves and I think, you weren't even there you silly cow.

put 'em up

Relationships are sites of winning or losing—not connection and safety, but dominance and subjugation. Every gesture, word, act, opportunity, kind face, sexual advance, dismissal, rebuff, celebration, rejection, invitation, advancement, smile, look, step forward or step back and every offered fee has to be regarded first as an insult, a threat or as a potential act of violence which is slowly neutralised. It is the only way to live a life, to regard anyone coming close as the enemy, as someone who is guaranteed to take from you, tokenise you, treat you as lesser because you are different.

The only way to have a relationship with the man I want to be with is through conflict. The only time he pays rapt attention to me is when I am splitting with rage or when I manufacture needing an urgent answer to an existential question about us. The war is waged like morse code, needle-bursts of pressure and silence. He renders me dead or alive with the flare of his attention. He is like this with all of us. He is a void and there is no way to fill it.

back of the line

For a decade there is a woman in Mallorca who the man I want to be with would see three or four times a year. The start of the end of this relationship with her overlaps with the beginning of the relationship with the woman I am obsessed with and all runs concurrent to the marriage that he says he sometimes forgets he's in. He tells me this woman in Mallorca was like a second wife. We are sat in a bar in Hoxton which we have found down a side street. At our table, there are large, heavy art books stacked under the glass. We open one at random and to his surprise, the woman in Mallorca's house is photographed in the book. He points to one of the pictures and says, when you curve around this corner there's a great view of the ocean, then points to another place and says, you can't see it but the kitchen is over there. A flatness settles over me. Occasionally, when we are talking, he will offhandedly say things like, oh a long time ago I had a fling with... and then mentions a student or a one-night stand with some woman he met at an event. My head snaps back and I say, but at that time you were with the woman in Mallorca and his face pinches and he shrugs. I don't know why I need him to be loyal to someone, perhaps so I can say to myself that he could be capable of it with me one day. The woman I am obsessed with overtakes everything soon after she meets him and it seems she ousts the woman in Mallorca or ensures she ousts her by demanding all of his attention. There is one Easter where he has three women in London at the same time, two of whom have flown in to vie for his attention. As he scurries between them, the woman in Mallorca becomes increasingly confused as to why he won't sleep with her and the woman I am obsessed with repeatedly calls him so he would drop what he was doing to meet her so she could be sure he wasn't with anyone else and he makes sure he's home in the evenings so his wife isn't suspicious. He says this was a stressful time for him. Through all of this, he has me waiting in the wings and three weeks later he starts something with me.

i can fix him

After their relationship disintegrates, the woman in Mallorca sends him letters to his mother's house. He knows when these letters will arrive because he receives emails from UPS, tracking their arrival and he intercepts them without any fuss. He reads them and sends handwritten replies back, doesn't address anything she says and instead writes of the weather. I want to know everything, down to the detail of how their meetings were arranged, what it was like to spend so much time together in Mallorca, did he stay over when she came to London. But I don't ask. I am burned up by jealousy that the woman in Mallorca had him alone for four or five nights at a stretch, jealous of their shared sleep. He tells me he fucked the woman I am obsessed with incessantly at the height of their obsession with one another, they just couldn't stop. He tells me she could come from being around him. He offhandedly reveals domestic details he knows about the woman I am obsessed with and my nose flares with everything he doesn't say about how he came to acquire such intimate knowledge of her. How can he know me when he's so committed to misunderstanding me. Once he withholds sex from me, I am allocated an audience with him three or four hours once every fortnight. He affords us no privacy—strained and formal, we always meet in a public place.

the math ain't mathing

At the end of a talk he holds in Copenhagen, there is a party for all the insiders. This is where he meets the woman I am obsessed with. A few months later, at a large private calendar event for their industry in a prominent foreign city, the woman I am obsessed with kisses the man I want to be with for the first time, with her then-husband in the next palatial room. When he tells me this story he says they always knew they would sleep together, there was a lot of chemistry between them. Later, when she falls out of favour, he recasts their meeting as her hunting him down and forcing him to be with her and telling me he regrets ever having met her.

There is a big cross-country tour in Spain arranged for the man I want to be with which goes very well. He's on top of the world. This tour somehow ends at the woman in Mallorca's glorious hilltop house where there is a party. This is where their relationship starts. He says she is loving and patient and loyal. One night over dinner he accidentally tells her he's bought a new flat with his wife, which flies in the face of the lies he'd told her that he would be with her, so she throws a glass of wine in his face in retribution. A waiter heading in their direction does an about-turn and later they laugh about it.

There is some trip abroad where he meets his wife, he is cagily protective over their story. He tells me he feels nothing for her and she is able to put up with a lot from him. Perhaps she hasn't left him because she does not have the self-esteem to leave or she can't leave because she is financially dependent on him or they really are like family and they are satisfied with living like brother and sister or very good friends, I don't know. Maybe she loves him and she suffers as I do. Nothing he says about their life together makes sense or it makes complete sense and I don't want to understand it. He says he wants children but they don't sleep together and he won't leave so perhaps he doesn't want children. He starts cheating on her three years in and twenty years later, hasn't stopped.

The man I want to be with is transfixed by his indecision. This is where the drama is for him, all grist for the mill, all these women waiting on his word and it energises him, propels him as he moves out into the world, conquering it with his ideas. He is hypnotised by his addiction to conflict, to the fraught and desperate attention of women pleading with their lives to be with him or to make up his mind, to the push/pull mechanics of flirting with and then refusing intimacy. He can hardly believe that women react to him this way and it fascinates him. We are all of us engaged in a collective self-harm by trying to love him, seeking to be loved by him.

first of all i didn't miss the red flags i looked at them and thought yeah that's sexy

I send a fan email to the man I want to be with. He replies and tells me to come and say hello at a talk he's doing. At the end of the talk I stay behind until everyone has left. He is still on stage so I take a deep breath, stride over to him and say hello. At the bar, he lets me buy him an orange juice. He doesn't seem to be too impressed at meeting me and I am a bit put off by him, he seems distracted and aloof and we scrap antagonistically. We lose contact for two years. He tells me later he's sure we will run into each other again. Our relationship starts when I send him an email saying, you may not remember me but I met you two years ago and then I ask him for a favour that requires him to meet me in person for a tour of a building. I am convinced he will not reply as it very much seemed like we didn't like one another, so I'm surprised when an email comes back from him within half an hour. He says yes. I am called to work very last minute and so I can't be there on the day of the tour. Someone covers me. When I tell him I won't be there, he says, that's a shame, the only reason I said yes to helping is to see you again. I am flattered and confused by his interest in me. He comes to the event celebrating his participation and yet again I cannot be there because of work. We run into each other accidentally at a screening and a protest. We intentionally meet twice in person and after emailing for a while, he tells me he has a proposition, almost a performative exercise. He would like to have sex with me. He is curious as to how we will fuck and kiss and am I not curious about that too? He writes, only this is on the table—no more. He'll give me some time to think about it and will be in touch again. He is everywhere and lauded and everyone wants him. People say his name like they're spending someone else's money. The proximity to power is too much to resist. I make my pact and immediately, I say yes.

roll me one

The first time I visit the River Lea, I am with fifteen of my wreckhead friends. We haven't been together in this way in a massive group since our early twenties. We are all thirty now and this group-hang is a reliving of those old days rather than their explosive discovery. We sit on the muddy bank on a patchwork of tiny scarves, crowded around one another with crates of tinnies stacked next to us and open cans splashing over our heads as we gesticulate wildly, talk and take the piss out of each other, half-naked, languidly unaware of our beauty. We swing rope into the water and swim down to where the river widens into a boggy marsh and back up again. When it's time to leave, we put our rubbish neatly on top of the overflowing bins, we hold our faces close to one another and say, this was nice, I've missed this, I've missed you. Our availability makes us equals. It is before the majority of them have children where their inflexible diaries denote adulthood. My childlessness and my endlessly empty hours mean I work around them, learn not to take it personally, the silence, the vague dates to meet up that go by or the missed appointments to call, and instead shrug them off. They have families and serious lives.

The next day I take the man I want to be with to the River Lea. The day is hot, so so hot, hot enough to make you miserable. The walk from Homerton station seems to take hours and hours, much longer than the day with my friends. He doesn't offer to carry the blanket I'm holding or the food I have for us in my bag. He has brought nothing with him. He is impatient and tells me he has somewhere to be, why is this so far away, he snaps, why didn't you bring a bike. When we reach the river, he points to the sign knocked into the ground with a warning that the River Lea is a poisoned river, one of the most poisonous rivers in London and there is a high level of rat urine and faeces in it. I had not seen this sign when I was with my friends. After jumping into the water, I had swallowed some of it and had cut my ankle against the bank but I have to be sexy and nonchalant right now so I say, who cares. We walk onto the bank and I look across the shaded canopy, the dancing light on the water and the hairy trees which trail and swing with the breeze, beautiful tattooed Hackney women stand in bikinis and talk to one another thigh high in the stream with their arms crossed, young children launch themselves off the swing-rope into cannonballs, competing over who can make the biggest splash. I lay the blanket on the muddy bank for us to sit on and spread my shop bought picnic out for us to share. He has hungry eyes like a crocodile. Watching from the banks of the river, he devours one half-naked woman then the next. I sit obediently next to him, waiting for him to notice me. I am wearing a sensible Adidas swimsuit and he is in a bad mood. I empty myself out in order to appear as his ideal, whatever it is, I'll be.

When I am back at my flat, my stomach takes a turn. I am sick for three days, the River Lea makes me shit and throw up and I move like an accordion around the toilet attending to whichever hole demands the most urgent attention. As I recover, I watch the entirety of an old series of *Love Island* on Netflix, two years after it's been broadcast and then google where they are now and look at how much work they've had done since finding fame. I am still ropey on the sofa when my boyfriend returns from a trip. That evening, as we're settling in to watch something, I stare at him. He looks back at me, pulls a strange expression and tells me I'm looking at him weird. Our living room turns green and I spin forward in time and a voice says to me, you have to leave him. I do the maths very quickly. I turn thirty-one this year, and I'm on a slide to forty. If I do it when I'm thirty-five it'll be dangerous for me and if that's the case then why wait, it has to be now. I thought time stretched out forever, I thought I had the rest of my life to make this decision but I realise I am on a clock and it runs differently for me. I am female. There was never much time and I've wasted so much already.

ding dong

The man I want to be with and I go out-out. He is staying over at his mum's and she lives a ten-minute drive from the flat I share with my boyfriend. At the end of the night, I book an Uber for us. He insists it takes him back first but I insist I am first, I say, I'm the woman, I should be first, he relents. The driver is really fast. I silently will the car to go slower. Throughout the journey the man I want to be with speaks to me in honeyed low tones as I uncomfortably crane my head down to reach his shoulder. When we reach my flat, he puts his mum's address into the app on my phone so the driver can continue the journey to drop him off. A couple of years on from this, when we are in a bad patch of him completely ignoring me, I think, won't it be a great idea to send him a letter to tell him how I feel. I am desperate to get some sort of reaction from him, he fades from me all the time, harder to hold on to than a wisp of smoke. I need a way to solidify it. I don't have his address where he lives with his wife but don't I have his mum's address? I go through the history in my Uber app and find the journey we took two years previous. I write a heartsick letter and post it to the address he inputted into my phone. It is overwrought, longing, like a teenager, like a crazed fan, filled with the kind of fervour which insists the pop star looked at you from the stage.

The letter arrives at the wrong house, the address he had put in my Uber app had only been an approximation. The letter is open by the time it gets to his mum. His mum reads it and calls the man I want to be with in a panic. She asks him, who the hell is writing a letter like this and sending it to me for you. She is afraid. She asks, how did this person get my address. She tells him to call the police. He tells her he has a stalker, it's being handled and not to panic.

Vulnerability lends authenticity to my voice and fills in for where I do not have the more formal backing of an MFA or the recognition of an award or the prestige of an eight-way auction publishing deal. I have an English degree yet when faced with the task of writing, I am almost adrift. I rely on autobiographical detail, I masticate my life, spit it out and decorate it on the page. No one can dispute my experience even if they might rail against the way I communicate that experience and this becomes my first line of defence—*this actually happened to me* can fight any accusation of the rough and amateur way I use the tools. What is the line between being vulnerable and prostrating yourself for a system that won't recognise you? The onus is never on the system to adjust its hardness, it's on you to shape-shift and acquiesce. Do I don vulnerability as a weapon against this culture?—*If you require me to be hard and harder to fight you, I will rebel by being soft like a jelly-beaned being,* but like anything, you need to be softer and softer to have the same impact. Do I weaponise my own pain and cause harm to myself by revelling in that pain, nurturing it, putting myself in danger to encourage it and then working it over by verbalising it for display, to show society, I am a human being and I feel pain just like you. Is this violence turned inwards, a knife in my hand, the weight of my body grifting down to the hilt?

The same story is told over and over by all of us. Our human imaginations are funnelled to think along the narrow lines of the algorithm—*if you liked that you'll love this.* The narratives open to us are the ones based on our identities as it is these stories that are market and social media approved. They have a numbing familiarity to them. We second generation immigrants have the privilege of self-actualisation.

We make sculptures, direct films, write plays, novels, memoirs and poems about not having a home, of trying to find a home, of being between two types of home, what is home, of how we all feel ugly, of the mixed relationships we enter into with white people, losing our language from a culture we had a tenuous hold of in the first place, we tell the story of being acted upon, we speak from the position of the victim.

For an algorithm not built by us, for a platform not designed for us to attract a cultural system which excludes us, do we commit further harm by performing our Otherness—by Othering ourselves for likes, for reshares and approval, to gain a following, to build a fanbase? What are the effects of this alienation, do we even care? Is the need for fervent fans a deeper expression of the fear of being anonymous because we know in an uproar there is protection. We do not want to disappear inside a nameless mass if Something Bad Were To Happen. If we remain part of the masses, we know we will suffer the double injustice of institutional neglect by the police or the justice system compounded by the original crime—like with our murder (Stephen Lawrence, Nicole Smallman and Bibaa Henry but also too many others) or a history-making miscarriage of justice (the Post Office scandal and Grenfell), the threat of deportation from the Home Office (the Windrush scandal) or stripped citizenship (Shamima Begum) for making a terrible mistake when you were a child. Are the cravings for a fanbase an expression of how politically powerless we really feel? Or is it something else entirely? Though we insist we are Socialist and Marxist in our ideals, is social media and our pursuit for fame within this structure not the purest expression of individualistic, Thatcherite neo-colonial politics where we transform into scripted individual brands, launching ourselves like start-up companies while masquerading as being 'in service' to our 'communities' by 'taking up space' as if by being true to ourselves, we're doing everyone else a massive favour?

The easiest route to build a following is to penetrate culture and the fastest way to do this is to tell them the story they want to hear—the one about our assimilation to whiteness or the abhorrence, or failure of this assimilation so white people with the keys to the castle can gasp and shake their heads and say, *I never knew it was this bad, it's [insert year] for God's sake,* and then will lower the drawbridge to let us in? We know succumbing to this will secure us the status we seek. It is how we can have a 'name', we can sit on the panels and talk about 'diversity', come up with earnest solutions inside historic buildings in front of a rapt echo-chambered public which will never amount to anything except feeling good about ourselves for how terrible we feel at the state of the world, it becomes the workshops we run, the books we write when we yell, *we know what Britain really is and you don't, buy my book to find out the Truth.* A fanbase is how we will get the advances, how we secure the invitations to prestigious awards, headline one of the smaller tents at the bigger literary festivals or one day maybe we will even get to cosplay at being a gatekeeper by becoming one of the judges of a well-regarded prize. We think explaining ourselves or justifying our existence isn't too heavy a price to pay to gain entry through those gilded gates where liberal artsy white people will tokenise us as a symbol of their ideological progress—they can think they are so exotic for being into your work, *aren't they so edgy, so underground* or else most likely they will tip-toe around us, deferential but still exclusionary, it's not such a high price for admittance to the cultural establishment, we reason. If we specialise in telling others *What The World Is Really Like: A Race Relation,* it's not really such a burden to spin these pornographic trauma ballads for a little bit of status. We are saddened by the knowledge that nothing really collectively changes but reassured by the thought that *it did for me on an individual level*, as we backstroke across the vast placid sea of righteous superiority.

Who exactly are we addressing our creativity to? What do we hope to gain? What does this do to our voice? Does it matter? How does performing vulnerability and being performative to win the stamp of authority that whiteness brings, warp our private, most secret self? Who might we be outside of this one-sided dynamic? We seek to affect the cultural landscape. We take on our parents' struggle as if it were our own while dismissively exploiting the privilege of self-actualisation. We are able to ask, who am I, a question our parents were never able to ask themselves—but have we ever stopped to ask, what exactly is it we want to gain access to?

business i know

The man I want to be with tells me that he can't understand why I am so unhappy, I am a happy person, always smiling, he can't imagine my being sad. So I decide to cry in front of him. I make a point of crying in front of him every time I see him, forensically laying out the innards of my sadness. I can sense the perversion of his cruelty held in his wonder of my tears. I cry on the Heath, outside of Pret, in the street across the road from the British Museum, outside another Pret, outside Tate Modern, in Soho Square, outside the Royal Festival Hall. I heave up salty, fat tears in buckets from the blue caves of my stomach to prove the depths of my love for him. Once or twice, I cry so hard I am unable to breathe easily afterwards, my ribs are bruised from sobbing and another time I am unable to swallow properly for a week.

and i tell you it's so

I want to be fucked and my boyfriend wants to make love. I ask him to call me a slut in bed. He tells me he doesn't believe the way I want to have sex is who I truly am. I instantly lose my confidence and submit myself to what he thinks I should be. I'm not sure if what I want is what I want. I am convinced he knows me best, better than I know myself and because I have resigned the power of my decision making to him, he must be right, I don't want to be treated like a whore, he's right, it isn't me.

I suggest to my boyfriend maybe I'd be more into it if he talked dirty to me—say anything you want, call me whatever you want, anything, you can do whatever you want to me. I want to be the cause of his loss of inhibition, I want to be the reason for his loss of control. He falters and says he doesn't want me to be submissive to him and he doesn't want to speak to me like that, he has too much respect for me to treat me this way. I fold my lips inside my mouth and look away. He tries once. I make pained, embarrassed-for-him faces as if I'm braced for a car crash which forces him to stop. He tells me he doesn't want to do it again as I'm not encouraging.

I want him to render me stupid when he comes close to me, I want him to believe he owns my body, to tell me, in graphic detail, all the things he wants to do to me, to tell me what I feel like when he's inside me, that I'm tight and wet and only for him, I want to be spanked and bitten and objectified, I want him to grit his teeth as I throw myself on top of him and ride him with my hair swinging over my shoulders and my back arched. I want to make his knees shake when I suck him and I want him to be a little afraid of the power I have over him, how hard I make him come. But we do none of those things.

Once every couple of months, it is quiet, non-penetrative, perfunctory and gentle, two seahorses nuzzling in the surf and then we curl around one another and go to sleep.

martine syms, ugly plymouth, sadie coles hq

Across a gallery space lit riotously in blood red, three split screens run rolling sets of disjointed footage. The video clips are of the artist's trips to the beach, of piling into a cab with her friends, the shows she attends, split-second shots of faces, an endless overlap of images and sound mimicking the way we take in stories on Instagram where you cut between dozens of peoples' days within a minute, keeping up with the narrative of the way their lives are presented—this one has come out as non-binary, this one is moving in with their partner now, this one went on a date, is looking for love, puts up screenshots from Hinge for their six hundred followers and makes self-deprecating jokes about themselves, embarrassed about their search in this automated time where an algorithm has to get to know you before a human being can—where the algorithm gets to know you more intimately through the hundreds of false start conversations you have about what your favourite colour is and how many siblings you have—this one puts up a video of their progress in pole and then shows you the move they can do now so effortlessly with text laid on the clip saying *time is everything! growth!* You hear people you don't know, in living rooms you'll never be invited into, preparing meals you'll never eat. The pace of Syms' video is erratic, jerky, disorienting but familiar. We're used to video being presented this way. In this type of social media storytelling there is no volta, no crescendo, no pay-off in the plot line. Syms isolates the everyday quality of this type of media and asks you to focus on it, to interrogate the fragmented storytelling where we present ourselves as the protagonist of our own self-shot movies, of the sharp clips of people talking, the tease of information before a big reveal, the soft launches of boyfriends, of the universal quest to find a place in the world through love and acceptance and belonging and success via the documentation of your late-stage capitalist side hustles and Syms presents it here, isolated on three split screens, cascading fireworks at the end which then loop back to the beginning again.

My boyfriend is with me because next to my erratic behaviour he can look like the wise, steady one even though he has no direction to his life. Next to me, he can be the paternal force, the one who holds reason, which forces me to hold the intuition and feeling. I need his maternal care but it is this care which closes in on me. I am a trapped animal. I am comfortable here but because I am trapped, I lash out. My friends tell me to speak nicely to my boyfriend, they sympathise with him, they worry about him when he has to deal with me in these moods where I speak down to him and berate him. I publicly mock his inability to fuck me, to dominate me the way that I want him to. This makes him less of a man in my eyes and so contempt oozes out of me when we are in front of people.

My boyfriend tells me he wants to fill me with arms and legs—he wants me to bear his children. He tells me if we have babies, I can go back to work and he can look after them because I am not maternal really and not knowing myself, I say, yeah, I love working, I can have them and you can look after them, I can go to work and when I come home you will have cooked and I go out and do the work and he says, yes, you love working, you can go to work and I'll stay at home.

take this

The Peach and I stumble home on the night tube and I am coming up from a mis-timed half pill. The noticeboard flashes fifteen minutes for a train to Brixton which feels like hell. I have made a grave mistake. I should not be Underground, I should be on the dance floor but I have punted a guess we will have sex so it seems worth it. I'm not sure who started kissing who first but we did and haven't stopped for hours as we career around a pounding techno night at Oval Space. As we kiss, two boys come up close to our mouths watching our tongues move against one another, spitting bile in our ears and saying, you aren't even lesbians why are you doing this to us. Their voices seem to come from far away like in a dream. I break off our kiss and realise there are two real boys very close to us so I push one of them hard in the chest. The Peach and I run onto the dance floor and I grind into her, she puts one arm around me, grabs my tits and reaches for my mouth with her mouth and her other hand strokes my cunt through my clothes. A security guard walks over and says, there's no way you two are this into each other, you need a man. Later she tugs on my sleeve and says she wants to go home and since she is staying with me and I might have the chance of fucking her, I decide to go too. My friends, having just given me the half pill, say nothing to me about my chaotic behaviour as I smash into them and tell them I'm leaving.

On the platform, I stare at the orange spots on the noticeboard and my chest feels full of planets having a party so I decide the only thing to do is to sit still and stare straight ahead. We get off the tube at Brixton station and when we are sat at the top of the night bus, I stroke the Peach's face to soothe her as she has a little snooze on my shoulder.

We get inside my flat and take our coats and shoes off. We sit on the sofa and I try to kiss her again but she's stiffer this time, I try to take her top off but she pulls it down, I try to undo her jeans to lick her, I want my tongue on her quite badly but she runs from the sofa and stares at me. I beg her to come back. She has told me that her boyfriend won't fuck her and I think I could remedy this if only she could sit fucking still. From the corner of the living room, she puts her head in her hands and says she's never kissed a girl before and what does it mean that she's kissed one now and I think, oh for fuck's sake, and tell her, it's fine, it doesn't mean anything, come and sit down. She looks at the ground and doesn't move towards me. The mood has changed so I call it a night, offer her my bed and I sleep on the sofa. In the morning, she leaves early, she's got to have lunch with her boyfriend and his parents. She stands at the edge of the living room and stares at me, she looks awful, drawn and guilty. I am quiet. Eventually she says, I have to go and I say, ok, without moving my mouth and when she slams the front door I think, fuck, work is going to be awkward tomorrow.

pound

I book a hotel room for the night of the work Christmas party. My boyfriend asks me why I have done this and I say, we all have, it's just in case we get too drunk. He side-eyes me but says nothing. I am not sure if the Peach is coming but we have exchanged texts and reached a fragile peace by not talking about what happened that night at the club. She turns up at the party. We circle nervously around each other. She is wearing a dress that clings to her curvy hips and her huge tits. Her body is as fertile as the banks of a river, I want to plunge myself into her. We take a photo together at the booth. She has her arm around me and I tip my waist to one side so I end up looking curvier than I am and we both have huge joke sunglasses on and our mouths open. We stay together all night, dancing and drinking, working the room. Eventually, the last train is due, an alternate ending where we could safely stay as friends hangs like low fruit. Looking at Citymapper I say, the last train is in fifteen minutes, I keep my eyes down as I add casually, or I have a room. I look up, she nods and takes her coat so I grab mine and we leave. We get straight into bed once we are in the hotel room but as soon as we are in the dark and under the covers, she turns her back against me. I am not sure if I can be close to her, why won't she let me in? I move one hand onto her body and she stiffens, I shuffle closer against her back, cupping her bum with my lap and smell her neck, she turns to kiss me but as I pull into her, she pushes me away. I am filled with poison, hissing at her with frustration. Why the fuck did she come back to my room. She kisses me to take the edge off my anger but I want more. I knock and slam and slap at the door to get her legs to open. She curls in a ball.

I offer the Peach to the man I want to be with, sliced up without the stone. I send him the photo from the Christmas party and he asks how it was and I am bursting with happiness that I have finally caught his attention and I type back we were all over each other, we kissed so much my mouth is sore. He is delighted. He sends me a photo of a woman he knows, someone small with dark curly hair and clever liquid eyes and he says, I have wanted to fuck this woman for years do you fancy her. She is beautiful but icy, I don't and I don't know why he is telling me this but he is talking to me so I say yes, I do and he asks me what I'd do to her and I screw up my face, my soul flying out from my tapping fingertips through my phone.

The woman I am obsessed with comes across as well put together
on Instagram, she has a carefully curated grid. She perceives herself to
be vastly talented in that Victorian sense of being well-accomplished—
able to cook, draw, paint, host, write, she speaks a number of languages
and has an impressive cache of artistic and cultural historical knowledge.
Her feed is a primary way to express herself and as a by-product, a way
of nourishing her fans, it becomes a morale booster. She performs
a necessarily charitable act like a princess opening the doors of her
home. She edits herself in such a way that she could be perfect—she is
sugar-free, meat-free, gluten-free, generous towards her friends, cherished
by them in return, animals are drawn to her adoringly, she posts links
to fundraisers on her stories, often decries politicians' inaction over
climate change and believes she has enough authority on Instagram to
tag the most recent presidential incumbent in her public messages of
disapproval as if she is an elected congresswoman and these tagged
politicians would write in her comments, *of course, we were so wrong we see
the light now, thank you for tagging us in your posts!* All of this confers upon
her a purity of character, someone who is a fighter for justice and
benevolently in tune with all beings around her. Her fans leave comments
on her posts complimenting her photographic composition, praising
the affection she has for the land, her use of light. Men are hopeful for
her, leaving her comments which say, 'a great chef and a photographer,
you have it all!' Or, 'you're beautiful and clever' or, 'is there anything you
can't do'. The teeth in my stomach rattle for more information about
her. I find out humanising details about her from the man I want to
be with who I press for specifics regardless of whether he wants to speak

about her or not. I don't really care if it causes him pain. He tells me she can only have the best of the best at all times, her rigid ideas of perfection put unbearable pressure on him. He says she likes being seen with him and wants to be publicly recognised by insisting they go to his industry events together so it jeopardises his life. He says, she's not like you, you're easy going. I don't think this is a good thing. She makes him buy her a dress from Jigsaw and I screech, Jigsaw! Who the fuck shops there but old white women and he says, I knew you were going to say that. He says he dreams of taking me shopping and buying me things and I am tempted but I can't because it feels like he's giving me money in place of love except I do want gifts from him because I don't get love but the *Pretty Woman* overtures are *tew* much. There is another part of me that wants to meet her and commiserate, like two weary war vets, compare battle-scars, engage in friendly one-upmanship and offer sympathy. I want to find solace in failing to get him to love me. I want to grab her arm in recognition and say, he did that to me too! And laugh about it, which would take the sting out of the humiliation. I want to get drunk with her, sweep her hair over her shoulders and tell her she's beautiful and she'll find someone else, that she doesn't need him and neither do I. I want to get angry on her behalf and call him a cunt. I want to spill out of the bar, walk her to the station and tell her I'd like to see her again if she'd like to and she'd say, absolutely let's do something next week, come over and you can meet some of my friends. After a time, we could say to one another, God wasn't that weird we went for the same man? But we would forget that's how we met because our friendship would go so far back and we would simply be happy we have one another in our lives. We have something real.

qanon and me

I spend Christmas in bed crying into my childhood sheets at my parents' house. My feet dig into the too soft mattress and I'm falling through the gap between where I am and where I would like to be. The man I want to be with isn't letting me in. The relationship is not revealing itself to be the springboard I thought it would be. My eyes are scratched and I am staring unfocused into the beige wall ahead of me, I think about how just days before we had swapped presents and he had said he loved me for the first time, he just didn't know what to do about me, he could see a future but he wasn't sure which way his life should go. When we parted, he had pecked me on the lips, smelled my neck as he pressed his pelvis into mine, checked his phone and then left me to go back home, a home not made with me. On the Overground train I pick over our messages panning for the slightest glint in the water that would convince me it was worth the wait, glossing over where he says he can't commit, he is stuck, it is impossible to leave his wife, and instead I hold onto his compliments which he gives me as cheap recompense for any structural changes—as if new curtains would costume or refashion a gaping hole in the wall, as if he is an estate agent telling me, yes you're cold and this hole is largely inconvenient—but use your imagination and pretend it's a window, just look at that view.

I've scoured the internet for photos of the man I want to be with and his wife, and compared them to his photos with me and you can see by the way his shoulder is tipped against her and by the tightness in his face that he's not actually happy, he's actually trapped, she's trapping him and the way he is with me in my photos with him, he's touching me and relaxed and we have our arms around one another in front of people, which means he loves me more as it's obvious he's happier with me. I conveniently forget the folder on his phone which has cute domestic photos of them together where she is smiling widely into the camera and at him and I dismiss the knowledge he deletes all evidence of me from his life calling me 'Laura National Trust' in his phone. It is not convenient to the story I tell myself, of our star-crossed and obviously meant-to-be kind of love.

The fervent, paranoid, obsessive behaviour exhibited from Trump's base, which was given lighter fluid during his administration is uncomfortable for me. The searching belief nirvana is over the horizon, that all the pain we are experiencing now is temporary and the time and hope we have invested will be worth it, deifying someone to an ideology that might provide a framework for all the ills, real or imagined, in our lives remind me of the desperate, fraught, blinded way of combing the world for clues I am guilty of too. I retreat into dreams of delusion where I think the man I want to be with is trapped, doesn't know how to leave his wife, really desperately wants to be with me. As I'm the only one he can confide in, my having more 'knowledge' than the others must mean he is more committed to me, the only one who gets him, the one who inspires him, his wife is just there to do the housework rather than look at the reality of the situation, which is that he is not going anywhere and we have all been deeply betrayed. Having a plethora of women suits him just fine. There are no codes, there is only the tyranny of ruthless selfishness wrought by weak and inflated egos.

abbas zahedi, ouranophobia, chelsea sorting office

Abbas Zahedi walks about sixty of us through his exhibition on Instagram Live. The show has been forced to close prematurely and the building is being sold off to property developers so the stream functions as a time capsule. Although I am lucky to have caught it in person, I tune in because I want to see the show through Zahedi's eyes. Rather than add objects into the space, he says he decided to explore the idea of transplantation, moving one or many things to another place within the building to frustrate or layer the meaning. There are two floors, the main floor is flooded with bright white light, a corridor saturated in red light takes you down to an expansive basement floor, which once functioned as the postal workers' break room. There is no guidance, no wall text, nothing to separate the artist's acts of intervention and what is part of the derelict building. On the Live, he tells us he removed the mirrors from the downstairs bar's back wall to expose the brickwork and glue patterns underneath. He also removed eleven large squares of hardwood from the bar and refashioned them into very tall stairs on the upper floor which now gives you a view through the high-set windows. He takes his phone over to a space on the floor where he lifted eleven squares from the parquet and flipped them to reveal their blackened backs. He says he placed the floor tiles in a reverse parquet arrow and pointed them towards the red corridor, which also points in the direction of Mecca. He tells us of his other small acts—tying a label with the Aquarius symbol drawn on it to a square of wood which is then hung at an angle from the ceiling, and of adding chain to the top of the door as you walk in. Moving through the slabs of white and red light into black is like passing through realms or a kind of initiation, the red bass throbbing from the heart of the building lures you down into the pitch blackness, akin to a death. Downstairs, the staff bar has been turned into a dimly lit altar where distorted chanting bleeds from the panels like a memory. The removal of the mirrors on the back wall reveals six panels and the ghost of the glue that held them there, three with black straight lines and three with white zig zags. Zahedi says it becomes redolent of a yin and yang sign and this is echoed in a macro sense through the blackness downstairs in the basement and the white light upstairs. When I had visited in person, Victoria and I shrieked back up the stairs in fear because why wouldn't two women react like this in a basement with no one around—but then, tentatively, we returned and it became a welcome oblivion. We were drawn magnetically to the altar, the evaporation of self meant you could escape the confines of the flesh and fill the room. The re-emergence back into the light had us blinking wildly, unsure what else to take in. It is through the Live where I learn more about the architecture of the building and how Zahedi has threaded meaning into everything like a poem. On the upper floor, the windows were high for utility and security, so no one from outside could look in but also so no one from inside could look out. The architecture was designed in such a way to prevent the workers from wasting productivity by daydreaming. Zahedi pans the phone across the top of the walls near the ceiling where several white windows are now filled in. He tells us Management would watch the workers through glass but due to the height, the workers were unable to look back, a surveillance which is echoed through social media and our governments. I learn that Zahedi's construction of the stairs is a way of overcoming the architecture, of putting bodies at the level of the managers and democratising the view out of the window in an act of revenge on behalf of the spirits of the workers. Transforming material kept in shadow and overcoming that which is hidden by making it something useful and rebellious in the light, the meaning of this reverberates within me. The building, Zahedi tells us, should be seen as a body but I see it as a metaphor for the way the mind works too. The show has a sexy confidence which is augmented by its supremely quiet focus. It is akin to being touched slowly by someone you want to be touched by, when you want them to go fast and of their slowing it all down so you pay attention. It's the moment where you delay gratification, withholding so you enjoy how much the other person wants you, savouring your wanting of them, of their release to the animal, experiencing a body outside of words. The refusal to fill the space with objects but to move and reshape, invites chance and the unknown through negative space—because is this not faith, believing in what you cannot see? Is this not what invites God? An experience at its most powerful when it is suggested or alluded to, when you have to put the pieces together yourself.

simp

When I come back from work, I find my boyfriend is sitting on the sofa getting high with his friend. When I see there is no food on the hob, I crash into the living room like some 1950s husband, thunder in my eyes and demand to know where my dinner is. My boyfriend gives my rage a nickname, he calls it the Hulk. When I start to goad him or humiliate him, he says, the Hulk's back, or, tell the Hulk to go for a walk. These storms will descend with no care for who we are with or what we are doing. I lose my temper during a walk on the Moors at inbetweenmas, his father and his stepmother watching on, tight-lipped, as I stalk him across the hills, hurling insults at him. I am simpering with the man I want to be with. He is cruel and cold, and then warm and close with frightening changeability. I give his cold side a nickname and say his split personality is like Jekyll and Hyde. Minute to minute I never know who I am going to get with him. Minute to minute neither does my boyfriend with me.

i like the world in my head where i can rehearse

i open the door to my bedroom and in my mind it's a busy restaurant. i look left and right and i can't see the man i want to be with. i walk over to the corner wall of my room and i speak to the maître d', i'm looking for the man i want to be with, i say to him, i arrange my features to look perky and upbeat, the clientele are Shoreditch House types but i belong here, i'm a well-regarded author with a glittering future, this is how i carry myself—people talk about me in reverential tones when i enter the room, i'm my own centre of gravity, someone sexy and up and coming but i also cross into fashion and music and i cherry-pick what i want to do. This is my backstory, this is my reality. The maître d' walks me over to my bed where i spot him—the man i want to be with—he's at a table, he has his glasses on as he reads his phone, waiting for me. i warmly thank the blank spot where the maître d' stands and sit on the edge of my bed for the table. The man i want to be with is overawed by me and tries to hide it but because i know him so well i see it. He asks me how i am. i say fine, a waiter comes over, i order a gimlet, the man i want to be with asks me if i would like to eat and i say yes and the man i want to be with asks for menus and i sit there like a lady. i brush my hair off my face with my left hand and he is struck, i don't know what he's looking at until i do—it's a gigantic diamond on my finger. This ring signifies i am now loved, someone wants me so badly, they are willing to put a stone that would sink a ship on my finger to have me. But i am so used to this feeling, of being wanted, of being publicly celebrated, of belonging to someone, that faced now with someone who couldn't bear to claim me, i forget i was ever desperate and lonely because i have been branded so searingly by love. i look at my blank finger which has my ring on it—oh this, i exclaim and hide my hand pretending to be modest but really a delicious tang of satisfaction unfurls in my belly, creeps languidly up my spine and shoots into my heart, i've hurt him and so casually. However, he has this entirely annoying habit of not showing he's jealous so he pretends he hasn't reacted to it, only it's like a bloody carcass on the table, the stench of my being loved by another steams between us. How is your wife, i extend generously hoping she looks even more old and haggard than she did when i was with him. i am glowing, practically nuclear in my snug corner of the world where i am loved, i own things and people—i have replicated my DNA sequence successfully with someone who wants me, who chose me, my life is filled with more and more and more and he says she's fine, he says, congratulations on the book and the film, i saw it, it's brilliant, i always knew this about you and i say offhandedly but with practiced modesty, thank you. He says he misses me and the waiter comes over with our drinks, i politely wait for the waiter to leave and i look down at my coffee mug which is also the gimlet and say nothing, or i say, of course you would, or i just look at him with the weight of the words i said in the past. You were right, he says, i regret it and now—he says gesturing at my finger, it's too late.

//OR

or i open the door to my bedroom and it's Bold Tendencies in Peckham which i've never been to but i know the layout from Instagram, i have music on to create the mood of going out-out. i move to my bed which is the table where all my friends are. i dance and they are all around me, i hug the air as i'm hugging them and they are hugging me, i push my bum into the wall as if i am grinding against them and then i stop and turn and laugh at the wall, one of them offers me a drink, some of them are sat down, i laugh at one of their jokes, i am smiling ear to ear, i am so happy, i am so happy. i am not wearing much and what i am wearing hangs off me perfectly. i like one of the songs that is playing, it's a dub track and i look up to where my desk is by my windowsill, next to the chair which is piled with clothes, and the man i want to be with is djing and he's looking at me, he is already staring at me, he can't stop looking and i do a half wave and turn to my friends by the bed, hiding my face in my hair and i say, omg, the man i want to be with is djing why didn't you tell me and they say, we thought you knew, what will you do.

// OR

or i am having such a good time, i walk with one of my friends to where my closet is and we're queuing for a drink and a hand lands on my waist and i turn around and it's him.

// OR

or i am having such a good time, i have my back turned to where the dj booth is, and my friend grabs me and says, don't turn around but the man you want to be with is coming over, and i say, what the fuck do i do and they say, act cool but also he's a dick, fuck him and i turn around and he's in front of me and i say, nice tune and he laughs and says, i thought you'd be here, and i say nothing just look glowing and happy because i am having regular sex and can afford facials and he catches my waist as he talks or he takes my hand and says, it would be really nice to see you and i say, yeah maybe and he says, can i call you and i say, sure and we talk and i tease him light-heartedly, it's all so light, it's all so heartedly, and i throw all the pain up in the air like juggling balls in the blue and shining sky and then i say, i have to get back to my friends because i want to leave him wanting more but really it's not that deep, i just don't care anymore and he says, oh alright, looks disappointed and says, i'll call you and i nod warmly but in a non-committal way as if saying goodbye to an old school teacher i'm trying to get away from and turn around.

// OR

or i open the door, it is the day we're meeting and i sit at my usual table on the bed at the café and i am early, or sometimes i'm finishing off a meeting, i've just snuck meeting him in between two appointments and it's just quicker if i stay where i am as i have to be off in an hour, i haven't said this to the man i want to be with because i'm so busy i forget to tell him. He arrives and we order a coffee and i say, i've only got an hour and he looks disappointed but i have an opening to go to with my boyfriend who i'm deeply in love with.

// OR

or i have a baby strapped to me, my loving husband has dropped me off. The man i want to be with and my husband and i have all cooed over the baby and my husband leaves us to chat, takes the baby, because he's so supportive and we're so open he knows everything and the man i want to be with says, that could have been us and i get really angry, or else i am calm but generous because he is lonely and heartbroken and finally i am not anymore, i am happy or i say, i always told you you'd regret me the most, or i say nothing or i say, it was meant to be like this i'm so happy now and hours and hours will pass.

I watch videos on YouTube where the woman I am obsessed with talks alongside her famous father. He's a poet, critic and advocate for the land who, in the late seventies, has early success with a seminal, apparently ground-breaking essay called *Seeking Poetry in the Growth of a Garden*. Soon after publication, he moves to England before returning to California in the late eighties where he buys fifty acres of land in Mendocino. He publishes several other poetry and essay collections in quick succession after this, the most notable being *Seed, Boundary & Air*, which wins him the American Book Award. He wins this highly regarded award the same year the woman I am obsessed with is born and I can see how this confluence of events creates her sense of herself, intrinsically tied to the quality and robustness of words. Ten years later her father publishes a widely acclaimed poetry collection called *Wolf Peak* and nine years after that follows with an essay collection called *Later & Now: A Call for Peace*. Her father's friends gradually move onto the land, seduced by nostalgia. He encourages them to build their own homes and to start their families. The farm evolves into a commune type growing community. Here they pitch in to help raise each other's children and together grow vegetables which are so bountiful that they become suppliers to nearby restaurants and birth the burgeoning food scene in the area as the increased quality of ingredients attracts some of the best chefs on the West Coast. In 2009 her father is awarded a MacArthur Genius Grant, which the woman I am obsessed with mentions on Instagram at every given opportunity. On the anniversaries of his two wins, she posts photos from the award ceremonies and her captions address him directly, which feels ridiculous as he's not even on the platform so instead she gathers the praise meant for him, for herself. The farm grows large in reputation and the woman I am obsessed with's father has a lot of influence. He leaves a team to run the day to day and now politically advocates for the importance of the health of the soil all throughout America. I've seen the sun-drenched throwback posts of him, where the woman I am obsessed with will write a caption celebrating how brave he was in starting something so revolutionary at a time when she says no one else was thinking about this. In the earnest videos where they are interviewed very deferentially, I notice she has recently started wearing colour instead of dressing like a middle-aged woman, which I think is a style intervention from the man I want to be with. Apple green and yellow look very nice on her. I watch her mannerisms, her gestures with her hands, her fingers splayed delicately like a woman in a medieval painting. Someone in her comments writes 'some people create art in everything they do and you are one of them'. She would be complimented for farting— someone would write, *I usually hate farts but when you do them, my god, so floral and unusual!* She is held aloft within a beloved centre which comes with class and money and status. These are things the man I want to be with has too though he still pretends he's an exile in the suburbs when he holds the world in his palm. The woman I am obsessed with had a premier education, really very stellar, she makes sure you know it by using very convoluted words I have to google. She advocates for change but only through the respected, formal channels like voting for the neoliberal Democratic candidate rather than supporting community groups in the margins as I think she is of the belief power has to remain in the hands of those who were born to wield it. Though she believes herself to be on the more Marxist side of the political spectrum, her imagination cannot actually stretch beyond the centre left. I am shocked to learn she can speak three languages, none of which she has a genetic affiliation to, it was something her father wanted her to be able to do. My mother speaks a colonial French called Creole, but I can't because my parents deliberately did not speak their languages to me so I would not be put at a disadvantage. They wanted to give my English every opportunity to be strong.

I watch how she long-blinks and then smiles, jerking her head into her neck, all simultaneously when she is very pleased and I do it too except I can't remember if I have copied her or if I have always done it. In the talks I watch of hers, I am hawk-eyed for any involuntary gesture she makes, I watch her laugh, she smiles widely, has a wide mouth. I watch her laugh as if she were a specimen of mine. When she is listening but trying to pose beautifully too, she pins her nose down and pouts and I watch her eyes slide to the screen to surreptitiously check what she looks like. When she is teased very gently by an interviewer, she pulls her bottom lip out to the side and grits her teeth and looks very sweet and naughty. When she makes this face, she could be someone I might be friends with because I too do this gesture (but did I copy her, I can't remember) and I wonder if this sweetness is what the man I want to be with saw in her for all of her pretension. I wonder what she looks like when she comes. She has a nice bum, not a flat white girl bum and that disappoints me. She is also very strong. I've deep dived and gone to the recesses of her Instagram and see she can do back bends and crow pose, things I cannot do. The man I want to be with told me he would like to pull my legs over my head but I'd have to be flexible and wonder if he said it to me, thinking of her. She says she has five jobs but when my dad had to work a second job at KFC to pay the mortgage, he didn't tell us or anyone because there was no pride in having two jobs so why can she say she has five, unless she has none? She stands on her tiptoes when she poses for photographs, she often poses for photographs in the same way as the man I want to be with, by frustrating the camera in some way—obscuring her face with an object, or with false modesty looks off to the side. I instinctively screenshot her selfies from her stories and stare at them in the early hours of the morning comparing them to photos of her face years before when he met her and against my face now. I don't know who he loves more, does he even love me. He tells me he came inside her with complete abandon. He very carefully and deliberately keeps our bodies apart.

it's all fun and games

The man I want to be with tells me he's thought about what he'd say at our wedding, he thinks I'd make a good mother. When I hold him to his words, he tells me he doesn't remember saying them or instead tells me, no what I said was, you'd make a good mother ~in general~. When I try to force him to tell me what I am to him he says, we are friends or we are more than friends or the more obscure, you are the sun. I am so furious when he won't define us, I send him a barrage of texts which makes him put his phone in his pocket and not look at it for a few hours until he's sure I've calmed myself down. I'm not even afforded the dignity of being called a girlfriend. The reality is, I am part of a chaste harem, a supply of crazed female attention he likes to disturb when he's bored but it hurts to admit this to myself so I put it out of my mind and pretend it is only the two of us and pretend he actually desperately wants to be with me and pretend he finds the situation between us as unbearable as I do and pretend he wants to resolve the situation because if I believe this then my chasing has a purpose. The day we find the woman in Mallorca's house in the art book at the bar, he pretends to put a ring on my finger and writes to me afterwards, I looked happy and for him it was intense, he felt his problems melt away. I take it as a sign. He says this to me occasionally, peering at a future from a safe distance but leaves me squinting toward the horizon unsure if the shimmer is water or a mirage. He speaks in possibility when I demand to know what he intends to do about us. I abdicate all agency. I assume his words will spear into action but they don't. It sinks into a space he calls the upside-down, borrowing the image from *Stranger Things*. We're a relationship-in-waiting and it's only he who has the ability to fire the starting pistol. Every day I think, this will be the day, he will tell me today he's going to leave all the rest of them and be just mine. The tension robs me of sleep and it is the only thing I can think about and the only thing I want to talk to him about. In order to fend off intimacy and body block commitment, he plays all of us off one another. What we know of one another we know through him. It's clear he doesn't view women he is romantically interested in as people and we treat each other the same way. I wonder how so many intelligent women who claim to be for women's stories and promoting women's lives and women's independence, can be this cut-throat and possessive over a man. In public we would all decry this behaviour, we would shout, dump him! to our friends. It's so archaic and humiliating to realise nothing has changed despite all the rhetoric suggesting it has. We will still turn on each other. What we should have done is unionise but instead we splinter. I live on edge and my entire life's energy is spent combing for clues, comparing his words to his actions and trying to track him online through the people I know he knows but have never met. At the beginning, he chases me with focused intensity. Over the course of the first few months, I give in to him, give up my scepticism and think, if he wants me this much and only this way, ok fine let's see what happens. However, as if aware of my softening towards him, aware the chase is over and he has me, he initiates gaping silences, he tells me to get in touch with him in a week, in a month. His absence becomes intoxicating and feeds my obsession. The distances mean I can fill them with whatever projection I want him to be. In my fantasies he could be the perfect boyfriend and the perfect father for my unborn children. The reason he hasn't left his wife for any of the other women he has on the side is because he hasn't met the right one yet. The fault is with the women, not with him, it's their fault if they think he has wasted their time, it's because they were not perfect for him. As I am perfect for him, I can afford to be generous and in conversations with him, I take their side more often than not even as I seek to destroy them. It is a way I can exhibit my exceptionalism and say to him, I'm not like those other women scrapping and fighting over you, I am reflective sanctuary. Here as goddess and garden I can wield a fragile superiority. Initially, he doesn't tell me his other suitors' names so I make up nicknames for them and then when he finally gives me their names, I launch them like they are ticking bombs, lob them at him to see what happens, to shake the fantasy it is just him and me. If I want to, I can pretend his absences are due to his work and his unavailability is not of his choosing and in his own way I have a kind of commitment—I have a seat at the table, I'm at least considered an option. He invites me to suspend reality and because it is better than realising I am hanging on with no guarantees I go along with it. It is punctuated by harsh doses of reality when I attend family dos and friends' weddings where alone and forlorn, I will text him, I wish you were here with me and he'll text back, you don't need me. I crave his validation but then will disregard it when I have it because I have to force it out of him. In an email sent when he's at an airport in Cleveland, between his having seen the woman I am obsessed with at yet another event I do not have access to and him calling his wife at home to smooth things over with her about a separate dispute around his family, I spit at him that on his deathbed he'll see my face and know he was wrong.

i start my day with a complex blend green juice

The woman I am obsessed with is at pains to always insist how communal her upbringing was. She says she was raised by a village, it was a collaborative effort to raise her, she had many parents. A community was not an oppressive system for her. The woman I am obsessed with lives in an abundant mindset. She wants more of everything. When she is away, she treats the area's local farmer's market like it's a trip to church and will lay her purchases out on her return home and show us, her adoring fans, what she's putting in that prized, white body of hers week upon week. She posts this weekly shop on the grid of her Instagram and she will get dozens of comments filled with heart-eyed emojis as if she has solely invented the concept of shopping for vegetables rather than do what we all do which is buy food without needing to tell anyone about it. Every morning she makes a concoction of green juice with about eleven different ingredients in it and adds collagen, mixing it into a beautiful handmade iridescent glass and takes a photo of it with a single circular ice cube, drenched in morning sunlight. She buys Wagyu beef and will demonstrate how she will wrap it in a dishcloth soaked with salt, red wine and herbs and roast it over a fire. The comments under this post all express urgent, alarmed concern for the sacrificed dishcloth and I think white people are wild for how they will have an acute empathy for anything bar actual melanated human beings.

The woman I am obsessed with has an older half-sister called Djuna. She and the woman I am obsessed with have different mothers and from what I can see they have a politely warm relationship. The split from the father seemed to be quite traumatic as Djuna alludes to it in the captions to her posts where she says, 'mum, so proud of you for raising me on your own'. She is based in London, is married to an architect and they own a portfolio of flats and studios. I click on the Architectural Digest link about the most recent build from her husband's Instagram bio. The woman I am obsessed with puts up a story with a link to the estate agent. I click through and the flat is a price on enquiry. They are colonising South London in concrete.

After seeing a friend in Ladywell, I think, it's not that far to their house and I'm only having a look, so I divert. It's on my way home, I reason. It's just by the station, I think to myself, I'm only popping over and then I'll be on my way home. I cross the road at the Tesco and walk down a mews. The blended complex of flats and studios look just like the photos. The exterior is mottled concrete and I can see inside because of the huge windows. They've decorated the interior with mid-century furniture so everything is old but six times more expensive than if you bought it new. Their buttercream sofa is by Mario Bellini and when the husband puts it up for sale in a post, all the people in the comments bemoan his selling of it, some expressing real grief, so they decide to keep it. As I'm looking from across the road, at the building, the front door suddenly opens and I see someone whose face I know very well. Djuna walks out with her toddler, battling a stroller. She is tall and has an expensive aura about her, it's almost the first thing I sense about her—the protective shimmer of money.

I think, it's not much to follow her now that I'm here, is it. She bends down to talk to her child, her name is Milo. I've watched her grow the last year or so. She looks like a dick. I get out my phone as if I'm lost as I do look suspicious gawping at them, but they don't really notice me. I walk back to the end of the mews onto the high street and I wait for them. When she emerges at the end of the street, she turns left and walks back up the way I came, with Milo bouncing up and down next to her as she navigates the stroller with one hand, her other holding her child's hand. I leave a large distance between us and watch them as they chatter like two friends. I've never followed anyone before and I'm surprised at how easy it is and how engrossed people are in their lives that they don't notice someone tracking them. I assume she's heading to the park as she often comments how she is revivified by the outdoors. Her sculptor mother lives in St Ives and needs the outside elements too. When they enter the park, I intentionally lose them as there aren't as many people to camouflage me but I watch them from the entrance gate. They stop on one side of the hill. Djuna pulls out a ball for Milo to play with, she eventually gets tired and sits down on a bench. She doesn't pull her phone out of her pocket as she's probably one of those technologically ethical mothers, but I bet she's dying to scroll.

I watch them for a while before deciding to leave them to it. I think, next time I'll talk to you.

i might look innocent but i screenshot a lot

Sometimes I think about what I could do for revenge. Sometimes I think about posting a letter to his wife and in it I will write in black sharpie, he's fucked the woman I am obsessed with in your bed. I am fixated with his capability to have done this and how it happened on the weekend he cancelled fucking me to fuck her. I want to know if he changed the sheets before he fucked the woman I am obsessed with to erase his wife, or did he change the sheets after to erase the woman I am obsessed with, or did he not change them thereby erasing neither because to change the sheets would be weird because why would someone who does zero housework suddenly change the sheets and did the woman who I am obsessed with revel in piercing the sanctity of their bed as she fucked him, was she more turned on because she was thinking of two people and not just one? Telling his wife still won't be enough to break them up I'm sure, she has stuck with him through so much already. If she saw my kidnapper's style note, he'd say to her it's vicious rumours, he'd blame it on a stalker he has, it wouldn't work. Sometimes I think I'll print off the emails where he talks about his wife and about the other women he was fucking—the ones she knows about. I would print out the emails he writes about fucking me, which she doesn't know about, I would kill him with his own words, but are printouts quite lame? I would have to screenshot the emails, scrub out my name using the tool on WhatsApp, send them to someone secure, save them and then print them off again because I don't know how to use Photoshop. Would my painstakingly arranged printouts make me look more desperate than I actually am? Like I've put too much work into it? I've seen the memes of the photos taken of women who have printouts with their ashamed boyfriends next to them in public. I would be one of those women. But on the other hand, is this not the best way to do it? He can be the misogynist and call us all crazy to his wife, we chased him relentlessly what else could he do but get his dick wet, he really did try so hard to get away! And she can be a misogynist and believe his lies—he was but a piece of driftwood yet what can she say to his words written down? He posts an envelope with his old address on an obscure blog and I screenshot and google it to see where it is. One day, we are walking aimlessly around a high street by a church when he stops, points up at a building and says I used to live here and I want to say with a roll of my eyes *~I know~* but I arrange my face into *~before gaining the knowledge~* by raising my eyebrows, then arrange it to *~after gaining the knowledge~* by gently nodding my head. I wonder if I can find his current address. I put his name into google adding 'address' and there it is, the first link, I copy and paste it into my Notes. When I post my revenge printouts, I could ask a friend to write the address for me because he might recognise my handwriting but then I guess he will know it's me from the content and do I want anyone else knowing I did this. I just want to anticipate him intercepting the letter and her not opening it. Sometimes I google her name, which I found by scouring the internet over a long period of time because I couldn't figure out if he was single or not but I did vaguely remember he used to mention being with someone and then I started to google it by adding 'email address' because I don't want to be beholden by chance, I want to make sure she really gets it but unfortunately it doesn't come up. When I ask him to use her name with me, I ask, what's her name because he never uses it, he only refers to her as his 'wife'—and then one day he says it and I think *~I know~* and then arrange my face into *~before gaining the knowledge~*

by looking straight at him intently, then to ~*after gaining the knowledge*~ by looking far off and hurt into the distance and then I say, will you please use it with me? Like I have any kind of moral high ground. I want to penetrate their intimacy where they use one another's names. Was she more important than me because he wouldn't use her name or was she less important than me because he wouldn't use it and would forcing him to use her name when talking to me mean we were all on an equal footing now? Would it be better to send off the printouts without an introduction by me? Is it a bit rude to send them with no context? Probably. But I guess she will understand what I'm giving her. I will enjoy imagining the cognitive dissonance of ~*before gaining the knowledge*~ where she opens the envelope, to the pause while calibrating it and then ~*after gaining the knowledge*~ which I can only hope will be pure hell for her but I know nothing will really happen to disrupt their life. He's done many bad things and she has stuck with him, what are my silly emails where he says, he doesn't desire her, would like to have children with me and I'm the most amazing person he's ever known and that he feels nothing when he's with her, going to do really? If they were that unhappy, her finding out he had two long-term relationships running at the same time as her would have seen to it, but no, they are still together. I put the address I find into Maps and see their front door on street view next to a fruit and vegetable stall that matches up with what he's described to me. At our picnic on the Heath, I bring a couple of slices of a courgette and lemon cake I baked and a flask of tea and ask him not to come empty-handed because the first time we had a picnic I asked him what he brought and he said, myself, yet this time he arrives with black grapes, unceremoniously dumped on top of a plastic bag, which have a sticky white film over them and then he berates me for not bringing water to wash them. I ask him where he got them and won't eat them when he tells me, saying rather mightily, pointing my nose in the air, that I want nothing of his life with her in my mouth, even though I let him kiss me when I fall asleep on the warm grass. Now I know where they live and weirdly was working not very far from them for a month, I get a slick thrill when I pass their flat. Early in the morning when I am on my way home from work, sun not even risen yet, I will pull up my car on their road, no—I will pull it round the corner with the hazards flashing or will that draw too much attention, will I get a ticket? No— I will pull up then I will jump out of the car and buzz their buzzer to shock them awake at half five in the morning—where is their bedroom facing and will he recognise me? Maybe I should tie my hair up and pull on a hood. I will buzz and buzz, I want to invade their living space, I want to destroy the hand that ticks, one comfortable second to the next.

before you get comfortable

The man I want to be with asks me along to a charity do he's been invited to. We are in a private garden with lots of other people. We are stood facing the same way so the length of our bodies are melded close, my back right up against his front, his knees locked right into the back of my knees, I can feel his dick hard through our clothes and I want to sit on it. He puts his arms around me and interlocks his fingers on my stomach as we talk to different people. I am in a kind of heaven. I make friends with a beautiful woman in a green dress with fish net stockings who takes a series of pictures of us on my phone as we try to pose for a photo. I am engrossed in him, looking at him tenderly as he pulls faces, then another photo, we are wrestling with our hands and laughing, in another he catches hold of my hand, we're both mid-talking but our eyes are shiny and we're smiling, then the final one we are in total full throttle motion, the background is blurry, we are the only thing in focus and we hold hands as if we are one person, his left hand connecting to my right, our thumbs wrapped around the other, the shape we make is one circle. We have the kind of happiness I've seen in couples when they are getting married but instead it's a Thursday and it's a do, for nothing in particular. He isn't in contact with me for days after this meeting. I am distraught. I go away with my friends and I cry and ask for it to be over, for this pain to be over, I can't bear it anymore. They say nothing and stroke my hair. I cave, unable to bear the silence from him. I text to ask him why he's so quiet, where has he gone and he replies he's in Norfolk with his wife and then travelling onto Basel with her but doesn't mention when he is back. I check the woman I am obsessed with's profile and I see she posts a photo of her father's garden and in the caption she addresses it and says I will miss you. Two days later she posts from Basel and I scream.

Perhaps I too selectively glorify the good old days, just different days to the ones that are being glorified now. Now there is the throbbing pulse of fascism, of monolithic thinking, of the fear of immigrants, of a culture, mean-spirited and backward-looking, of a government wanting to reimagine the country as a floating tax haven, of worshipping only money, gutted and cultureless, unfettered by a population who has any critical thought only ultimate fandom, where holding politicians to account is repackaged as hate, hate is repackaged as love and the love is one-sided and slanting.

what's it called

The thing is I don't even hate-follow the woman I am obsessed with, I don't follow her at all. I don't follow her and I hate her—what's that called?

when you miss your man that's not your man but can't trip cos he ain't your man but he is your man

On the bus I google 'track phone' and an array of links fly up.
I click on the first one and it has a taskbar which says, enter number. My
heart is sick with longing. I enter the man I want to be with's number.
My thumb hovers before pressing 'enter'. A pop-up flashes saying I must
register my details on the website. I close the tab. I look around me
to check if anyone can see I have done this terrible thing and behaved like
a poisonous female, like they always say we are—trying to track a man
down. I open WhatsApp and look at the last time he was online as a sign
he is alive and breathing. It is a betrayal. He is connecting with other
people, just not with me.

nepotism it girl

I live in the world of mass consumerism, picking out
kitchenware and furniture from Ikea, pining for jewellery from Argos
and showing off fast fashion from the high street. One size fits all is the
perfect size for me. My race blots out my individuality quite neatly.
I am in the world of identical goods with in-built obsolescence. The
woman I am obsessed with will only ever be an individual, the uniformity
with which mass consumerism and race engulfs me does not touch her
universe. Her regenerative organic food is grown to a level of purity by
which she can sneer at the quality in Whole Foods. Her food is grown
by farmers she knows by first name and arranged in beautiful, handmade,
one-off pottery. Her food can be traced back to the seed, whereas mine
is bought through a complex line of anonymised, automated, industrialist
networks. Every object she owns is of heirloom quality, made by one
person and has an individual personality. They often come from makers
who have disclaimers like *due to the handmade nature of these items some of
them will differentiate in tone, or texture or colour, but we think it adds to their
specialness*. Sometimes the makers are dead so immediately the object
becomes more special in her care, or they are sourced from antique
shops off dirt tracks from abroad. As the child of a famous person, this
feeling of being a rare kind of human being born of a rare kind of
human being, from a uniquely wrought household is underlined by the
objects she surrounds herself with. Even the books she reads are first
editions or out of print, sourced from ramshackle bookshops in out
of the way places from cities all over the world. The unattainability
of what she chooses to surround herself with seemingly rubs off on
her. It further alludes to qualities she has that are innately hers by

birthright and it creates a kind of frenzy around her from others. The woman I am obsessed with captions her food as 'pure', 'perfect' and 'best'. Only this standard of quality will do. She presents nettle-infused risotto in saucepans called *donabe* which I have to google ($500 from an 'authentic' Japanese vendor), wild flowers she buys from her local farmers market are presented in handmade designer jugs shipped over from her half-sister in 'England' (she says *England* in this very deliberate way, not mongrel 'Britain' or the 'UK', but *England* as if she has extracted the native character of the country that is mine). Her food has individual character, she anthropomorphises her pink lettuce captioning the photo with 'this gorgeous beauty is coming home with me' as if even her food has to look devastatingly alluring, has to have some remarkable individual quality to it before she deigns to bring it home with her. In an interview, she says she spent almost $100 on eight heritage apples and it is obvious she was unaware of the problematic nature of admitting this, which implies she doesn't know the value of money divided by industrial bodily labour and time. She posts very simple recipes and people write comments like 'doing this now', 'thanks for the idea', 'where did you get that beautiful pot', 'this is the recipe of the year'. Under her photos, people will write 'you have such a wonderful sensibility for arranging still life, utilizing natural light and framing photographs', and I think, if the only thing I had to do all day was take a photo of what I bought at a farmer's market then my photos would be a still life too. Hatescrolling her Instagram unleashes something corrosive in me. I sneer as I read through the sometimes hundreds of comments she gets, the adulation, how carefully she is spoken to, my mouth gets used to the shape it makes when reading them, relishes it even. She surreptitiously deletes anyone who questions her cultural appropriation of her espousing other cultures like it's her own but because I am often first to her posts or stories, I see them and then because I revisit her profile so often, I notice them disappear. When I see this, I crow with glee at her inability to bear being criticised. To my delight she poses awkwardly in her selfies. She has a smile frozen to her face and the whites of her eyes are too exposed giving her a frightened look, her hair is flipped to one side often using a filter, always preferring her left side. She tags where she buys her clothes, a balloon-sleeved peasant top with a wide prairie collar tapering off to a frilly cuff paired with plain white jeans from companies I haven't heard of, owned by white women who pose in beautiful minimal interiors. They want you to buy their goods but their material diet is one of abstinence. I google the price of her clothes and total that her outfit costs about three thousand pounds. The company that sells the top have this frolicky white girl cottage core aesthetic. In June 2020 they post a black square and from then on, they post frolicky Black women in the company's cottage core aesthetic and say they acknowledge they have to do better. I meticulously research each item she recommends in a tastemaker list she is included in. She buys vintage designer clothes from high-end boutiques, plain clothes and shoes from expensive, independent designers who use their full names on their labels.

I wonder why no one questions her on the nepotism she benefits from, I see it all as one system, this self-congratulatory circle of back-patting and unaccountability, a circle of whiteness that commends their open-mindedness but the kind of open-mindedness that looks just like them, a hall of mirrors in a closed room. I hover over the items she tags and recommends thinking, this is a way of getting close to her. If I buy these one-off items like her, from individual vendors, from makers who have limited edition runs of their very niche specific items like clay candle holders, or jugs, or plates, then I too will be a unique, rare and special person like she is and maybe the man I want to be with will want me and won't throw me away like he does so dismissively. I will be something of note and care. I will be something to show off owning.

a stranger in the city

I am sitting on my sofa in the flat I share with my boyfriend. He is away for a couple of nights and I am alone eating a family-sized portion of Bolognese my mum has cooked for me, which she put in Tupperware the last time I went to her house. I go for seconds. I eat past the point of being full, I eat until I can feel the food at the base of my throat. I am laying in the middle of the sofa with my legs up, my belly popped out, propping my head up with two pillows watching something trashy. I often get texts or calls on my phone from numbers I don't recognise offering me work as the industry I am in is small and there is a tacit agreement this happens. Having to go to strange spaces around the country at short notice is normal for me. I have work the next day at five in the morning which came through via this method, someone I've never met instructing me to arrive in a place I've never been to before and I am fretting about missing one of the early morning shuttle buses scheduled to leave from my flat, which does about three stops and then goes fast into town. My phone pings, I pick it up. An email from the man I want to be with. It is the very early start of us and he has barely touched my life, a week ago he told me at some point we'll sleep together but not now, not yet and it makes me want to sleep with him when I'm not even sure I do. In the email, he asks if I am free to meet him but not to email back, to text him instead and he provides a number. I text the number straightaway and I say, you mean now? yes I can meet you. I look at the time, it's coming up to nine. He emails again and gives me an address, he says it's a hotel in East London. He doesn't offer to buy me an Uber. I call my boyfriend and tell him I'm going to sleep so he doesn't call me. I am out in ten minutes, I wear a pair of Lycra leggings and a backless top, no bra. I haven't waxed my legs but that's a problem for future me. I am out so quick I am nearly sick because I am so full. There is never a moment I think being this available is a bad thing for me. I reason, a main character would go, a main character says yes to life.

In the cab over we text back and forth to establish some kind of connection because we don't have one and now are going to be thrown together. I don't know if I'm seeing him for sex but I know I am curious about him. The Uber turns into a street I haven't been down before and stops outside a building with a blank face. I check Maps and its little red pointer indicates I have reached the hotel. There is no sign over the door, it looks like a house it is so discreet. I get out of the cab, look up at the building. I'm here, I text the man I want to be with and he replies, come up. I can't see the entrance. I walk past the hotel three or four times and it's later and later and I can't work out how to get in. I am out of kilter with my environment. It feels like my body morphs into the spaghetti arms of Mr. Tickle. He texts, what's happened to you, you got here ages ago, and I reply, I'm still outside I don't know how to get in, he says, there's a buzzer. I pass the building back and forth, slower and slower until eventually I see the buzzer out of the corner of my eye so I stop and I buzz. The man behind the small desk in the tiny reception area has watched me ping from side to side while studiously writing on a piece of paper refusing to lift his head. I cross the threshold and walk the four steps it takes to reach him and finally announce, I'm here to see the manI want to be with. He picks up the phone and calls up to the room. I feel really grown up and an electric thrill at saying his name out loud to a stranger, at the link now forged between him and me as if it makes me a more important person. The man at reception tells me the room number and says, it's up the stairs. I walk up and get lost in the rabbit warren of corridors but find it eventually and knock on the door. The man I want to be with opens it, I say, your takeaway has arrived. Over the years I will run this over my mind and think, that quip could have been much funnier, I could have found a funnier joke and I still think of what could have been a better thing to say but haven't found it yet. I enter the room and he has the television on BBC1, there's a small sofa at the base of the bed. I take a seat to steady my legs. I ask him why he's in a hotel in London, why isn't he in his flat and he shakes his head and offers me a drink from the minibar. I ask for a gin. I am too loud because I am nervous. He is trembling like he's done a lot of coke but I don't think he's high, there is a lot of twanging energy about him. I look at his phone on the table beside me and his screen is smashed, I say, can't you afford a new phone, and he doesn't say anything back. We flirt and argue until midnight about things that don't matter, it seems like we don't much like each other. I think it's going badly. I stretch my legs out and he looks at them like he wants to eat them. I look at him looking at them. I don't think a man has ever looked at me like this before. I am immature for my age and unaware of my presence in a room. I think I am invisible and nothing and ugly and here is this very important person giving me attention. He looks at me like I'm a piece of meat and I like it. It's getting to the point where I need to leave or fuck him and I don't want to do either. It's midnight. I play "Black Sea" by Drexciya from my phone connecting it to the vintage looking radio's aux cable. He is sitting on a chair and I am kneeling on the floor by his feet and I say, listen to this and look up at him. He kisses me quite suddenly as he realises if he doesn't, nothing is going to happen. I know now that this is unusual for him, to make the first move like this. He kisses quickly, too quickly and keeps his mouth too small, I try to slow him down but he wants to go fast, fast, fast. He says later, kissing me was like being swallowed, my mouth is too big. We kiss on the small sofa with the TV off and I am very reluctant to kiss him but I do because he wants me to kiss him and I want him to like me and I'm curious as to where this is going to go but I'm not sure enough about him to fuck him so I kiss him. He wants me to come to the bed and at one point, from behind me lifts me up from my armpits to haul me onto it but I am too tall for him to do that so my shoulders climb up to my ears and I don't move and I pull a face like a disgruntled cat. I say I don't want to come to the bed because in my mind then I'd really be cheating. I haven't told him I have a boyfriend and I can't figure out if the man I want to be with is single or going through a break-up as I sense there is a heartbreak suffered somewhere recently though he presents like a bachelor and yet I feel sorry for him and I want to make him feel better. I go to the bed and my clothes are off quite fast but I keep my knickers on, he doesn't seem to mind the hair on my legs. I want him to feel good and because he seems sad, I swallow his cock, taking him into the back of my throat, he groans. I place my body across his to block my face with my back because I don't want him to see into my eyes or what I look like as I'm doing it. His cock is beautiful and I fall in love with it. Sucking him is like I am swimming in cool, clean sharp water and I hold my breath and dive inside until I can hear he is close to coming, I bring my head up for air and grip my fist at the base of him, put the tip of him back in my mouth and make his cock very wet, my tongue meeting my fingers in a quickening rhythm. When I feel him twitch, I lift my lips and I watch him come into all my saliva and my tears and my sweat and my hand as I slip my fingers up and down. He has his eyes closed, I watch him as his nose and his mouth twitch like he's being released from pain. When he opens his eyes all the nervous cokey energy has evaporated. He takes a deep breath. I hold my hand off the bed so as not to wet the sheets. His cock lays fatly on his leg. I haven't done this in a long time. I want to please him, and I sense his release afterwards is like I've taken a great weight off him, and I am glad to be able to do this for him. I ask again why he's in a hotel room and he tells me an ex, an American he has been trying to get over, has come back to the country. She has a boyfriend and although it is complicated, they love one another, he just doesn't know what to do. He tells me he has a wife, a two decades-long marriage—someone he's not told me about. He says he doesn't wear a ring because it irritates his finger. His wife knows about the woman I am obsessed with and she hates her, he had promised not to see her again but he has broken this promise several times. He says, that's not all. He says there are other women he flirts with over email but hardly ever meets and then there is also a woman in Mallorca, someone he's been with for the last decade. He tells me all three women know about one another now and he is caught in the middle. He says he's not sure he can love anyone. He fell in love once a long time ago with a woman I later call the Egyptian woman, I don't learn her name, he says he couldn't leave his wife for her and so he has written his heart off and I should too, don't fall in love with me, he tells me, I'm dangerous.

Processing the information is a torrent of displacements in the timelines in my head—so he is going through a break-up, he isn't single, this is not the beginning of a love story between me and him. Not that he asks but so that he knows, I am also embroiled in a relationship with its own political landscape and there are claims too on my heart, I try to assert myself by telling him I am in a long-term relationship and we love each other and I am happy but unsatisfied but he's barely listening. I am overwhelmed with all the things he tells me, but I know my place now even as I struggle to reconcile myself to it—I am merely a speck and distraction from this other drama and from these adult women who loom large in his imagination. I feel like a child in a room full of grown-ups and they're having conversations above my head I can't participate in and I don't understand. I start to feel awful, rejected, used, ridiculous, so I slide off the bed and say, I'm going to leave. He says, ok, you can stay if you want, but I think to myself it is too intimate to sleep next to him, it would serve to highlight the distance between us and how much of a stranger he is to me plus I need my things for work. I go to the bathroom to wash my hands, then untangle my backless top and put my clothes on. He walks the short distance with me to the door, says goodnight and closes it behind me. I walk through the corridor and down the stairs at half two in the morning and sit outside the hotel on the curb quite stunned and unsettled. I wish I had thick eyeliner running down my face. I wish I was wearing leather. I wish I was wearing fishnet stockings that were torn. I wish I had red lipstick smudged across my face. A man stops near me and is smoking. I ask if I can have one. Wordlessly he passes the packet, I take one, he hands his lighter and we smoke in companionable silence. My Ubers keep cancelling on me as none of them want to go to South London. I have to be up for work in two and a half hours. I feel like those girls from the movies who have dramatic lives in New York. I wonder if having sex like this means I'm a grown-up now. The man I want to be with doesn't look down to see if I'm ok and I know this because I keep looking up to check. Fifteen minutes later I am in a cab and my phone buzzes soon after we set off. The man I want to be with texts and he says he understands if I don't want to carry on with this after everything he has told me. I text back straightaway and say, I do.

The next morning, I email him because I don't think he would want me to text him. I wish him good luck going home, he says, thank you, he's about to head back now. I have to position myself as the friend because it seems it is the only spot open. It is romantic elsewhere. He wants a platonic place to time-out so I decide this is what I'll be. I text him a few weeks later to see what happens and what happens is the message bounces back. He's changed his phone number and not thought to give it to me.

rumpelstiltskin

The night he gives me her name is the undoing of me. Really, it's the only thing I have left of him. It seems like the only real thing this man gives me is her.

i dream the man i want to be with is in the body of my boyfriend, i am in his flat. His wife is sleeping in the next room and i think, shit he's crashing around he's going to wake her up. When i join him, the man i want to be with is out of the body of my boyfriend and is inside his body. A loud alarm goes off, so he disappears downstairs to fix it. His wife wakes up and i hear her moving about the flat so i hide behind the door. She walks to the room i am hiding in, stands in the doorway with her hands on her waist and her legs set wide and she says, oh it's not you is it, and says my name. i push the door open and i say calmly yes, it is, it's me. We talk and i say to her, why do you hate all the women he's been with, why don't you hate him, he's the one who's done this to you, it's not us and she doesn't have an answer. i am struck by paralysing crushing terror at the thought of having him on my own now and not sharing the weight of him with her. i don't want him to leave her, i want him to stay put. She leads me into the kitchen. It is a very white room with skylights, it is so bright. i sit on a kitchen stool and we continue the conversation. His wife is praising me in some way saying i am different to the others and i interrupt her and say, i have to be honest, i'm in love with him so i'm not objective here. i realise there is somewhere i have to be, i have to leave. She puts her hand on her heart and she says, you are always welcome here.

          i have another dream. i am in his kitchen with two men and we are talking of work. We all stand up. The two men leave quickly. i am by the doorway, i draw a breath. His wife comes in and squeezes in very close to me, she doesn't look at me, she has bags and bags of food shopping. When i am in the stairwell i hear her speaking warmly to

him, cooing and bringing in gossip from the outside world. i am on
a bicycle, relieved to be out of there when they both appear to my right
from a side street riding on bicycles too. They are behind me and i hear
their friendly talk, they laugh a lot and chatter about their daily business.
i hang back so i am behind them when they pull their bikes into a shop,
she goes in and as he waits outside for her i hiss at him, this is nothing
like what you described it to be between you. He shrugs. My heart aches,
the flatness descends. There's nothing more to be said. i cycle off.

we'll save questions until the end

The woman I am obsessed with is doing a talk over Live with the woman with the popular YouTube channel. They are talking over one another. The woman with the popular YouTube channel is hosting. I am sat on the floor of my parent's living room. The comments ping in, complimenting the woman I am obsessed with for her father's advocacy, on her taste in beautiful objects. The woman with the popular YouTube channel introduces her this way, imbuing her with ethereal qualities by the taste she has in the precious things she surrounds herself with. It's all very cosy and nice between them, two privileged white women talking about care of the Earth and the land as if they are distinct from the white people who are racist and those who have pillaged this burning, now volatile planet of ours. Maybe the answer is not to buy less but of higher quality, maybe the answer is just not to buy things. The individualised, curated and careful consumerism they both espouse is like trying to solve the problem with more of the problem.

I notice they are not listening to one another. The woman with the popular YouTube channel says, mmmmmmmmmmmmmmm, very loudly and the woman I am obsessed with ploughs on regardless of the questions that are asked. The woman with the popular YouTube channel occasionally interrupts the woman I am obsessed with, reading out the comments from the people watching. No one critiques them. Resentment pinpricks my eyeballs. I think, I will write something in the comments. This feels like a transgression of my own shadowy rules, to be unknown to her but I want to rebel against this. My mouth takes on a tang. In the comment box I type, you're both talking over one another, you're not even listening to each other. The blood rushes to my ears and they start to pound, I wait to see if either of them register it. When the woman with the popular YouTube channel reads out my comment she does so in an automated way, reciting the words. When the meaning hits her, she says, oh, and pauses. The woman I am obsessed with jerks her head in surprise and there is a small, stunned silence between them. It's as if I have sliced them both very thinly. I have ruptured normal scheduling, I have disrupted their comfort. The woman I am obsessed with says, oooooohhhhhhhkkkaaaayyyyy. The woman with the popular YouTube channel laughs loudly, makes a *these peasants!* face and then they regroup and carry on. After my insertion, the woman with the popular YouTube channel moves and speaks more self-consciously and the woman I am obsessed with is more considered with her answers. They stop interrupting each other. I am literally high. I have penetrated into her universe and it makes me swim, makes my temples throb. I wait to see if the video will be posted online because I will watch it again before bed but they pretend it never happened. I laugh, which turns into a cackle, my eyes water, tears streaming down my face. Unknown furies lodged deep inside my rib cage make me stand up abruptly and to cope with all the additional energy, I hop from leg to leg, my phone an anchor in my hand.

mocha

How to force Djuna and Milo to talk to me in the park without it being completely weird? A mate of mine tells me that she hires a dog through BorrowMyDoggy so once a week she can feel something and now she's really good friends with the owners. It's like they have decided to co-parent a baby the way they have arranged things between them. I think that's what I should do—borrow a dog and walk it in the park near their house but I need to pick one dog and do the same thing, co-parent a pet so I can take it out whenever I need to. I sign up to the website, put my most approachable photo up as a profile picture, write a description that says I like the area and nature and outdoors, put Djuna's postcode as my postcode. I find a six-month old cockapoo called Mocha not far from their house. The dog looks like a literal toy, there's no way anyone could not stop and talk to me with a dog like this, there's no one that would think someone with a dog like this is anyone who would have bad intentions. I message the owner, Leah and say I could take him for two or three hours during the weekdays. The website comes with a caveat that you might not get a message back so I will take it as a sign not to pursue it if this is the case. I don't want to try too hard or push this too far. There are days of silence, so I think that's that then. I check the website absent-mindedly while I'm on a work call, click on the messages button and see an envelope flashing with a notification. Leah has replied and says we could arrange a phone call, she likes my profile, I seem amenable and warm. I reply straightaway, a phone call would be ace, it would be amazing to be able to sort something before the week is out and to my surprise Leah replies back, well as we're both online do you want to do it now? We speak on the phone. She is quiet and professional, and her dog is polite and loves children, which is perfect for me. I tell her I am freelance so work irregularly but when I'm not working I like to have a point to my walks and some company. We arrange to meet the next week, I decline her first offer so as not to look creepy or too eager. After the in-person introductory meeting, I appear safe and Leah says she is happy for me to take Mocha out for a walk. I've timed it so that I can boost it to the park to see if Djuna and Milo are there. I tuck Mocha under my arm and charge down the high street. His warm body is comforting and grounds me as my mind starts racing. What do I say to them? Do I mention the woman I am obsessed with? Do I keep it brief but memorable? How do I not overstay my welcome? How do I make myself someone she has to know? I have to slow down once I get past the gate to the park so as not to look too intentional. I don't want to look too intense. I drop Mocha down on the ground and we mooch around the perimeter of the park, past the pigeons pecking round the bins and the parakeets who screech overhead. Mocha is actually adorable and very curious. I wait for him to finish smelling things before we carry on walking again. A couple walk towards me, the woman starts to say, ohmigod he's so cute, really high-pitched and she crouches down to pet Mocha with her boyfriend standing and smiling at them both. The woman makes cooing noises and asks me what his name is and smiling back with just my teeth I say, Mocha. My eyes are distractedly looking around for Djuna, I don't think she's here but I'm also afraid to look. Mocha is excited and jumps on the woman and she starts burbling with laughter and baby voices and says, I want to take him home, with big Disney eyes at her boyfriend as if I will hand over a stranger's dog to this stranger and yet I think, this will work, what a great idea to get the world's cutest dog, this is so definitely the way to force people to talk to you in the street. Am I really going to do this? I have to dress nicer, a bit more tailored and muted but of quality, find Djuna and maybe put this plan in action.

i'm proud ov you

It takes me a long time to realise that when the man I want
to be with tells me he likes being seen with me in public what he means
is, he enjoys what my skin colour says about him to other people.

sneaky link

The man I want to be with tells me he is stuck and that I should protect myself against him. I ask him if he's happy with his wife and he says, happy enough, that's the problem. He tells me, you don't need me, you're young and full of life, you should live it and I will be there to champion you but don't rely on me, as if he's selling something back to me that I already own. Baring my teeth I tell him, I need commitment to continue talking to you and emotionally supporting you, I do so much for you, what the fuck does she do for you except take your money. I think, I am young, I have eggs, I can incubate life for him, I can give him a better life, one filled with sex and threesomes and babies and laughter and pride. He would get to walk around with me in public and my relative youth and my comparative beauty to his wife—why wouldn't he be with me, by having me at his side he would look better, why wouldn't he pick me. I do not hear he is releasing me. It makes me cling harder. He tells me he gets something out of his marriage and he cannot give me what I want. I need to keep hearing him reject me. I am unable to see what is right in front of me, I refuse the reality of it. I see his rejection as merely a first offer and keep going. He tells me, maybe you should take a break from me and come back in a month or two but maybe that's not a good idea either as you'll be coming back to this, I want to know what you're up to and I'm interested in what you do but there is no more. I spread my hands over the words. Even though they are in the plainest English, it's as if they have switched to hieroglyphics. I cannot take in their meaning. I search and search and dig down looking for some other reality which will serve up my dreams and fantasies ready-made of what my life would look like with him. I want to be rescued and so I retreat into delusion, what he really means when he says he can't be with me is that he wants to be with me, he's just scared so I need to fight for us, for the both of us. In this way, I relinquish control over my life and avoid growing up. If I blame him, I sidestep taking on the responsibility my life has not turned out to be the way that I wanted. I can always point to him and say to others, to myself, well I wanted children with him, and he didn't give it to me so that's why I'm a failure, it's all his fault. I want the illusion rather than my self-respect. I want to believe that there is a hidden meaning behind what he says so when he tells me he can't commit I think, he just means he can't commit *yet* because the blind conviction of my feelings overrides his knowledge of himself and what he's capable of giving. What he is, is greedy and lazy, selfish and a coward but what he also is, is clear and when he gives me a way out, I refuse to take it.

viennetta really is the epitome of luxury

I see my relationship with him in capitalist terms, like I'm playing the stock market. I throw good money after bad because I've thrown so much already what's a little more. I am owed profit, growth, a reward as I have given so much, I am an early investor, I deserve some payback for my loyalty. At what point do I get a return on my investment? My people-pleasing, my co-dependency, my lack of boundaries, which on the surface looks so giving, nurturing and self-effacing is actually controlling, ego-driven and emotionally demanding. There is something at the core of me that starts to warp at the fear of impending bankruptcy, grows ugly and distorted every time I slap a hand on the table and roar for what I believe is mine.

What is taste? Who determines the architecture of taste? What kind of person are you to be intimately invested in acquiring antique Welsh stick chairs to accent a room, or to deliberately curate an association between said chairs and your personhood to other people, to be the kind of person who other people say of you when you're not there, *oh they have such good taste*. Who decides these things? How do you acquire this knowledge of how to strip a room back but still convey luxury? What does it say about your person when you know what these desirable objects are? What does it say about your femininity if you know how to make a room pleasing? Knowing how to make a home is the ultimate wreath to crown your femininity. Where do you attain the confidence and the certainty to impose and expand yourself and your tastes onto four walls of a room and what does it say about you when you can't do this? What if the objects are there because they are functional and not to inspire envy in others? Where the chair you buy is to be sat on, not to be looked at and not sat on because it is too precious to be used or where the addition of your body will jeopardise the value of the object. How do you know how to elevate your life to art, something to be admired, envied, aspired to? Aren't these wealthy aesthetes on Instagram merely another iteration of a class elite deciding what is good and what is not good, shaping our reality the way they always have just better disguised by technology which has the optics of transparency and democracy? Are they not the beneficiaries of the old, covert systems, descendants of the children of settlers and the children of Empire, left-leaning spawn from right-leaning families, who can pick and choose objects plucked outside of their cultural context in some sort of static menagerie in order to show how innately open-minded they are even as their wealth has been drawn from global structures that decimate the cultures those objects are from? If only we could all be buffered from exploitatively neoliberal regimes by family money and luxuriously austere domestic settings.

gimmie

I want power and connections and money and status and access and influence I want to turn down invitations to events so elite they are called Cultural Moments—*you just had to be there darling*. I want to be ambivalent. I want brands to send me their limited edition drops with a pleading note to please wear the swag. I want to write a caption with an embarrassing blend of personal anecdote and brand name-dropping with #AD. I want verified celebrities to write over-familiar comments under my casual Tuesday night lobster rolls like, *coming over now, how did you make this, you always make food look so good*. I want to be flown in for talks at big events. I want the press to flatter me and seek my opinion on shit that bears no relevance to me, I want to *do* London Fashion Week, I want collaborations with galleries and labels, I want my presence to add charismatic allure to their events and they know this and want it. I want six figure advances, I want my writing to push the *cultural conversation*, I want my books to sell out at bookshops, I want to be on a second or third print run in the pre-sales. I want to be eagerly awaited. I want to be superficially humble about my incredible success, I want to wear it carelessly, I want to sell the rights to my book for TV, I want A-listers fighting each other in the streets for a chance to be attached to the script. I want to dangle myself in front of the papers, say, I don't know... *I think I want to maybe retire from writing, I want to focus on other aspects of my life*. I want them to be aghast at the destruction this will wreak on the cultural landscape, I want a hungry press, hungry for me, rather than jumping for scraps of attention like some rabid dog scrabbling around in the pit of my stomach desperate for someone to listen to what I have to say.

crawlies

The man I want to be with has a visual discipline of leaving behind scant evidence of himself. He seeks out mass gatherings so he can disappear. He is the quality of mercury, hard to hold the harder you hold on. Rather than participate himself, he chooses to observe, becomes an audience member and this is mirrored in his relationships. He stands to the side of our love for him, at a remove and handles us as if we were objects, things he has no emotional attachment to, no vested interest in, so it makes it easier to put us down and walk away. There isn't the exuberance of affection you could expect from a man being with a youngish woman who is really rather too keen on him. It is very Victorian, to have all of this sexual energy pent up, to be chaste, or it's tantric, it never climaxes, it's actually the most boring affair by virtue of having none of its hallmarks. I sleep with him five times spaced over six months in hotels dotted about Soho and near Kings Cross. I feel very grown-up having sex in hotels and lying to my boyfriend about having meetings to attend so late into the evenings. We do not have sex for connection, we have sex for release. My mind cannot retain the memory of our meetings but the fact that I can barely walk afterwards or open my mouth because I was so deliciously sore means my body retained the memory of the physical act even if my mind could not. I don't come with him. He is not interested in making me come as he feels it is my responsibility to make this happen for myself. My orgasm hovers at the edge but never envelopes me. What I enjoy is having the full glare of his attention on me uninterrupted for four hours, which is why I want to keep doing it. Our meetings develop a routine. He collects the key and pays for the room ahead of time, then he meets me in a nearby pub where I have a gin and tonic and he doesn't touch his beer. When we gain access to the room, he showers first and after brushing his teeth with a tiny travel toothbrush, will leave quickly afterwards but this softens over the months and the last time he walks me out of the hotel saying, I actually had a good time, maybe we could meet for lunch and I am proud as if I have graduated through some personality test. Down the lift, he talks to me of the woman I am obsessed with, how she plagues him and how sad he is about it. When we turn onto the street, we bump into someone he knows. If his acquaintance had been two seconds earlier or we had been two seconds later he would have seen us exit the hotel. The man I want to be with introduces me by the industry I'm in, as if to signal to the acquaintance that he and I are in a working relationship. I shake the man's hand. The man barely looks at me so keen he is to talk to the man I want to be with. There is a low-level state of jeopardy fostered when arranging to meet him. I am always certain it will be cancelled. I am held in the eroticism of my triggers. The day before one meeting, he emails to tell me the woman I am obsessed with has sent him a package and she insisted it had to be to his home address. I now understand this need to penetrate and disrupt his home life. He writes we might not be able to meet now as I have to wait for the postman. He does not want his wife to find the package and this is the only way to make sure it doesn't happen. I am tense as I wait for his verdict and a resentment towards this woman stews, why can't she fucking let him go, it's over for her, it's my turn. He emails me again later in the evening and says the package has bounced back to the woman I am obsessed with, she copied the address incorrectly but she's sure he gave her the wrong address. She's called him a cunt on the phone. I am relieved. I think I am very sophisticated for how calmly I accept all of this.

I think it's very French of me to have a lover who has lovers, to be able to use the word *lover*. It's very grown up of me to appear to be cool and detached while this post office whore gets irrational and angry. When he is sure there will be no further obstructions from the woman I am obsessed with, he confirms the meeting with me. I email back, she really has a knack for cock-blocking me and he writes back, indeed. When I daydream about the sex with him, my body jolts and my cunt flexes, I miss exits driving down the motorway yet I never resent the seven odd miles it adds to my journey. I email him and ask him when we are meeting again, he emails back and tells me he will check his diary. As he never books the next date in, on the 'date' we're on, our potential next meeting is left suspended. I think it is on me to keep the momentum going but really it is the way he wriggles out of responsibility for how hurt you will eventually be—because *you* kept arranging to meet, *you* were never forced, *you* initiated all the contact. As soon as I can rely on a monthly/bimonthly physical relationship with him, an escape from my comfortable but staid relationship, it disappears. It coincides with a family tragedy of his so I attribute it to that but it never comes back. After a respectful time has passed, I jokingly ask if we will sleep together again but he is so awkward and evasive, I don't ask again. There is some level of humiliation I can't entertain, heaped on all the other humiliations I can entertain, of seriously asking a man to fuck me and his saying no. He rations pleasure and the withholding takes me outside of the faculties of my mind. I am driven into the hands of some other force inside of myself who hasn't ever had the reins before. I am not sure if it is malevolent. I do know it likes to know things by any means necessary, it is ruthless, and it will put me in danger in order to be satisfied, it is as sinuous as the inside of a mouth, it has muscular strength like a tongue. That there are hordes of other people who might want the same thing as me, sends me into a near frenzy. I want it so no one else can have it. In the not having, it remains absolutely perfect, in my imagination it would fulfil all my needs, I would never need anyone again. I want it so that in the luxury of having it, I can ruin its perfection and then reject it when I am sure it means nothing. I want to succeed where all the other women failed, and it is not so much to win him as it is to defeat everyone else.

When I do not have access to his dick anymore but I have his number, I am mostly reduced to nagging him or crying or anger or self-righteously and hubristically insisting it will be me he regrets. He tells me, flaccidly, that he understands the effect his toxicity has on me, and he wants attention off me like he's a child. When he sends me this text a green, creeping feeling takes over me, a large caterpillar is crawling about on my skin, it tracks the goosebumps which flare up after my hair is raised. I text back, I don't want to be your mother, I want to fuck you, that's made me feel ill. He tells me another time that the pride he has in me is like that toward a daughter, the closest he will have to experiencing parental pride. I doubt he has ever said this to the woman I am obsessed with, they were so sexual, why have I been moved to the realm of family? Once he stops the sex, the escape from my real life is abruptly blocked and without my knowing it, I become enmeshed in a relationship which although is erotic with promise, is celibate, like my relationship with my boyfriend but unlike with my boyfriend there is no kindness and so I'm double-gated within something I do not want again.

dream

I daydream. I daydream constantly about him. I want the man I want to be with to change. I send him podcasts, quotes, screenshots, videos nudging him in the direction I want him to go in. I fantasise and fall in love with a version of him I'm not sure exists outside of my imagination. He is constantly failing in comparison to this person I know he could be. If he could only stop being exactly who he is, we could be happy.

We meet up in Shoreditch House where I have written up questions in pink biro on a plain piece of paper. I am interrogating the man I want to be with about us as if I were interviewing him (which afterwards he says is a format he likes.) He tells me how funny it is to like two women who are so opposite to one another, at the same time. It is so funny. I bite my lip because there are actually more than two of us and I can't trust what it is I am going to say. At this point I am trying to come across as chill? Like I'm absolutely chill with everything that is happening because it's chill? As if demanding better behaviour or putting down boundaries would mean that I am not chill? And I want to be a cool gal? So I am without boundaries and watchful instead.

We walk to the Underground. He tells me he doesn't know what it is about her, but he can't let go. I let the words burn the skin on my body as I mutely accompany his stream of thoughts about her. The things that drive me crazy about her are the things that drive me crazy about myself. She needs to be admired constantly, she needs praise and can't stand criticism, she wants to be seen as gifted and unique. I realise after ripping her book from somewhere so deep from google the bots must have commended my IP address for the commitment I showed to finding it, that she is a whirling, hysterical princess in the same way I am. I expect people to do things for me in the same way she does, she cannot leave her parents the same way I can't, she can't have the man I want to be with the same as me. I'm her bitter and twisted sister.

Online, I watch the launch of her book which she announces as if it's the Big Bang. She is interviewed by prestigious bookshops, she gets a spread in print (in print!) in *Harper's Bazaar* magazine, does

Instagram Lives with premium designers, gains 10K followers in a matter of weeks, is reposted by influencers and other big hitters with huge Instagram followings. She has an A-lister post her book on their grid (on their grid!) and she has very recognisable names in her corner of the book world lend her quotes to promote it. I read her prose and I am not impressed. It is overly wordy, unself-aware and leaves me with a buzzy head as if I'm in a thick fog but I see the way friendships with the right people, connections and a publicist can open the correct doors, where I have had to bang them down and celebrate the smallest of wins. People who are only figments of my imagination or else removed by a million degrees of separation, who would have a sort of polite forbearance if they ever met me because I am a member of the masses, know her by name, greet her warmly—she would be invited as a guest into their homes.

it not me

We are at a member's house in Soho. The receptionist instructs the man I want to be with to sign his name in the guest register. The man I want to be with picks up the pen. As his eyes scan down the list of names, the pen hovers, poised to meet the page. He sees something, a name. He puts the pen down and says someone up there knows his wife, we have to go and he leaves.

The man I want to be with does an about-turn on the woman I am obsessed with. During one of our regular bouts of not talking, he flies over to Tokyo for a work trip (which his wife is aware of) and then flies to Paris (which his wife is not aware of) to join the woman I am obsessed with because she refuses to fly to meet him on his terms. She wants to see him but for him to come to her. I can never make him do anything and it exhausts me, this power she has over him. I realise they were planning and anticipating this trip through the summer he was seeing me in London and my heart contracts. How does he have the time to do all this. How does he fill my entire life and I am only a sliver of his. He and I meet a couple of weeks after he has flown back because I have been unable to stay away from him for the forever that I threatened him with the month previous. We are in one of those gorgeous dark, wood-panelled pubs in Holborn. It is mournful outside, the sheets of rain are like a veil, the sky hangs grey and low which chokes the sun and casts a looming light through the small windows. I am wearing an outfit that is trying too hard because I am constantly auditioning for the part of his girlfriend and he is wearing an outfit that isn't trying at all because he wants everyone to leave him alone. The pub has yellow lamps on all the tables giving the room a warm, old London glow like a Hogarth painting. He tells me he has decided he no longer wants to speak to or see the woman I am obsessed with anymore. I jerk my head. The man I want to be with opens Instagram, gives me his phone and says, you block her. I narrow my eyes with suspicion but I don't hide how happy this makes me. On his phone, I go to her profile and press 'block account'. It is like killing her. The teeth in my stomach start their clattering. I ask him why the change of heart and he says she showed him her book and he couldn't stand it, that this was all there was to her. I told you, I say and he replies, I know you did. He tells me he and the woman I am obsessed with were at a party together and he saw someone who knows the circumstances of his life. The man I want to be with knew this person would casually mention to his wife they saw him at a party he wasn't supposed to be at with a woman he's not supposed to be talking to anymore. He asked the woman I am obsessed with to leave with him. She said no she wanted to stay so he spun on his heels and left without her. He says he tried to get hold of her for the whole next day before she picked up and eventually agreed to meet him again. He's never tried to do that with me. I'm never that unavailable to him. I wonder what I would have done in her place. I know I would have left with him to help him save face, I wouldn't have made him sweat a whole day. I couldn't have gone against what wants to devour him within me. I'm in awe of her, of her self-possession. Good for her, I say. His fingers drum a beat on my thigh as he looks out of the small windows at the grey sky, at the rain that pounds relentlessly onto the pavements. The story of the trip doesn't add up and I don't believe this is all that happened over there but he never says any more except to say how glad he is to be free of her.

A weird thing happens. After this severance, I switch sides and I start to defend her, I am protective over her when he speaks of her. I say, there's no denying she's a cunt but you led her on what else was she supposed to think you were going to do when you 'came inside her with abandon'—I quote his own words back at him. They struck me so forcefully when he first said them to me that I can't help setting them on fire and kicking them back at him. This phrase which he says so offhandedly is stuck on a loop, seared into my brain like a core memory, hard evidence of the way he is not in thrall to me the way he is in thrall to her, proof of how close he allowed her to get to him and how far away he keeps himself from me. I continue, of course she thought she was going to be with you. He stops drumming my leg, looks for a way to change the subject but I don't let him. I want to protect her and hurt her just as I want to protect him and hurt him. I'm not sure what I actually feel towards her anymore, all I know is I want to possess her in some way, even possess her absence. I wish he'd never told me her name. I wonder if the girl after me will talk of me to him as I talk of her. Will she scour the internet for meaning and patterns the way I do, will she compare her face to mine, will she obsess about all the ways she is lacking in comparison to me. I wonder if I will have enough cultural capital to keep her awake at night.

The woman I am obsessed with revolves herself around her father's garden and his farm. It is an embodiment of their philosophy of good food, interconnected community and an apparent deference to Mother Nature. In interviews she says as a child she picked peas and ate snails and was left to wander around freely amongst the herbs and lettuce and vegetables they grew in their backyard in Mendocino, free to discover what she calls the natural world. She says this wild place developed her sensorially, making her acutely attuned to the rhythms of growing, of patience, of taste. She says her father picked the type of flowers to grow not for their appearance but for their smell, for their history and connection to an older, more honest type of living. Her father planted fruit trees to give them hard nuggets of kumquat and quince, an ancient, gnarled olive tree anchors the centre of their garden that then unfurls into miles and miles of fields. The woman I am obsessed with is celebrated by others as being embodied in a way which has been lost to us industrialised cretins. She is looked up to, as if she and her father alone could lead us back to the Garden of Eden, so lost we are to the storm. She says she can strip even an urban environment of edible plants she can forage and name. Every landscape has the possibility for nourishment in her capable hands. She is elemental and runs on animal time.

I do not know anything about the land, about plants, about growing things, about seasonal food. I am used to all-night corner shops blasting their vegetables under fluorescent lights, supermarkets that provide flavourless consistency by flying in produce at all times of the year. I am used to pre-packaged food wrapped possessively in plastic, of chicken shops studded into the high street and the fatty immediacy of Deliveroo. I am transplanted here to this place, to this country and I am only of this place and this country. A history I do not know occurred to move me here, I don't really know my story. I wish I had a connection to land, to native plants and soil and earth from which generations before me were born. What I rely on is the falsity of concrete and cement.

The woman I am obsessed with is not native to America. Historically she is the immigrant. I watch her talk online about her father's poetry, his advocacy and his way of living, the only authority she has is rooted in being the perfect embodiment of her alternate upbringing. She espouses the values of stewardship, of taking care of the land, of the importance and necessity of farmers. Her lack of awareness of being a white woman borne of a white man in a country baked in the violence of European colonialism, dictating values that were and are already being practiced by Indigenous people before they were forcibly disinherited, is the way in which liberalism separates itself from the systems of racism and genocide and from the structures that organise the way the world benefits particular groups over others. It is the ripping of the Indigenous people from the land and the land being continually pillaged for neo-colonial profit which has the climate spiralling into catastrophe. The West's insistence that it is humans who are an antithesis to the Earth is short-sighted and incorrect. It is a certain kind of human built into a particular system whereby solid, physical things like ancestral land, a tree, the rivers, water and rocks become unreal next to the dreamt up, magical apparatus of the stock market and quarterly growth. What is defined as 'real' has become abstracted—fuelling a disassociated state where we destroy without considering the consequences. As native people are pushed to the edge of existence, so have gone the way of the animals and the plants and the weather. The woman I am obsessed with's father's ethos is based on a carefully curated definition of wildness whose central premise is a false sense of what is 'natural'. What her and her father reap from the land is what they have grown with intent. What seems like an accident, of stunning visually delectable plants growing over and amongst each other to look like their house emerges from tangled ruggedness has had months of ruthless planning, clearing, professional garden landscapers brought in with maps, hours of debate over the choice of this seed over another, teenage trees imported and planted into the soil, which in time erases what is native because no one can remember what was there before. This green fairyland befallen at their feet, the carelessness of a stunning array of rare plants offering their fruit to her bestows a Demeter quality upon the woman I am obsessed with. She presents her relationship with Mother Nature as if she is her one borne descendant, as if she were some precious vaginal pearl. The woman I am obsessed with's fans coo and fuss and gasp and say, *thank you for sharing this with us, thank you for bringing us serenity,* when she posts her father's roses which she captions, *if only these photographs were scented.* All I see is the disinheritance and the bloodshed which runs through the land to have made it a quiet and safe place for her, a place of nourishment and sustenance— not a place of abject grief.

and. or. not

The woman I am obsessed with eats as if the world watches her eat, she eats as if being observed politically—there's seemingly no drop in standards. What she publicly advocates is privately adhered to, a rigidity that is only able to be accommodated as she has the time to be so discerning. Perhaps what I want is the stability of mass-produced food. When so much of life is tumultuous and uncertain and scary, perhaps being at the behest of the seasons is not something I want to experience because then there are yet more decisions I have to make, more money I have to spend. Perhaps what I want is knowing I can have tomatoes at any time of the year because I know how to cook four things very well and this ingredient is the staple to all of them because I work long hours and I don't want to have to look up how to cook new things in accordance with yet more restrictions on my choice when I have so little control over my life anyway. Why should I be bound to time when I have to give up on so much already. Perhaps I want the cradle of the lack of taste and flavour from my twenty-four-hour supermarket. What if I don't want something wholesome, what if I want something tasty and bad for me, a treat to allay all this drudgery, something now, quick, fatty and delicious. What if it is experiencing something good and fresh that has become the more traumatic thing. I do not want to be awake to my deadness. I want to remain asleep.

standing stones

I can drive to you down the A303, I say and he says, ok. I get stuck in traffic so I am a little late but I text him as I'm driving and tell him I'm not that far, twenty minutes at the most. I'm thinking I could drive him home and we could be in the car together for the remainder of the journey—finally! Some alone time! He emails me, don't, don't come, there's no point, I've already left, turn back, I can't see you. I slow to a stop, turn the car around in a small lay-by and with the engine revving stuck in first gear, email him back, ok though it would have been nice to see the sunset with you.

tender

My boyfriend sears a steak on a hot griddle pan and serves it with steamed dark green vegetables when I come on my period to make sure I have my strength. In the afternoons, I place my hand on his forehead to help him get to sleep quickly when he wants to have a nap while I have a cup of tea and watch *Gilmore Girls* until dinner. It's my favourite thing to help him to sleep well. We have a secret language and the same nickname for each other. I like the smell of him. In the mornings I bite the rolls of his neck, they are so juicy. We cram in together on our Freecycled corner sofa, watch box sets and eat junk food and massage each other. He takes the knots out of my jaw and presses the pressure point in my thumb to get rid of toxins. He makes me mash when I am sad without my saying, he'll just know from the texts I've been sending and will go out and get potatoes. He is out of bed before I am and in the mornings on the weekends, I run over to where he sits and he lifts his arms up and sings "The Most Beautiful Girl in the World" to me and I dance on the spot. He is totally invested in everything that happens to me and tells me I can do anything. He picks up the phone when anxiety attacks mug me in the street of all my decision-making processes and calms me so I can carry on with my day. I love his dad and get on really well with his mum. Our home is a refuge for our friends, they call it heartbreak hotel. When the world is cruel to them, they stay for days in our spare room and we feed them back to health. We are the mum and dad of our group, the head of the family, all my friends are his friends, and our life is inextricably linked.

don't/look

The man I want to be with and his wife become a warning sign for the kind of life I could be in for. I could turn out to be the man I want to be with in all the ways I don't want to be, living a dishonest life, sneaking in affairs and my boyfriend turning a blind eye to keep me.

green light

The man I want to be with has his head down as we're crossing the road. He is complaining about the woman I am obsessed with. He resents how she feels entitled to his time and disapproving of how unfaithful she has been. He wonders out loud what kind of person could behave that way, have no loyalty, cheat constantly. I glance at him and screw my features up as if they are meeting in the centre of my face. Are you serious? I say, you should be thankful everyday those two women decided to stay quiet about how you treated them, you should be on your knees in gratitude, they could have ruined you. He turns his face to look at me.

shadow boxing

After her most recent birthday, there is a communication blackout from the woman I am obsessed with. She usually posts a photographic deluge of her day, you would know when she took a shit she documents to this degree. She reappears a week later and then it's only stories made up of reposts which isn't like her. She's all about that OG content. I think, this is weird. I go on her boyfriend's Instagram and he's thrown a party but she's not there, I check the Instagram pages of the friends tagged in his stories to make sure she's not there and she isn't. Two weeks later, she posts a photo from a new city, she's in Marfa in Texas. The photo is of her back, her body language is collapsed, she is dressed all in black like an office worker on a lunch break after pulling an all-nighter, or like Darth Vader in the sand. I wonder if her and her boyfriend have broken up. She rarely posts in this time. She is then permanently with one friend. They go away for a month and she announces to her fans she is taking a break from Instagram, they all bid her *adieu*. I have withdrawal and want her to get back quickly. When she returns, the red ring around her profile photo makes my body lurch with the cortisol and I click through her stories. She's done a road trip through the Southern States. I scrutinise what she looks like, is she happy. I figure, she is definitely going through a break-up. I cackle and say, good, out loud to no one.

Now that they've broken up, the woman I am obsessed with's ex-boyfriend has taken to posting a series of nature photos on his grid. Hobbies you are obsessive about when you are on your own. When staying in seems like a kind of accusation.

The woman I am obsessed with announces she's decided off the back of her book and the thousands of likes and hundreds of dms she's received for the recipes she posts on Instagram, she is moving from Mendocino and opening a café in Marfa. She says she wants to live in a place with artists, she wants to fundamentally fuel artists' work in a way words can't—by penetrating their bodies and she says she will utilise her father's farming techniques to provide the ingredients, as much as can be, will be grown in a plot out the back. The ethos will be simple and seasonal. She wants to make it destination dining for the city art-crowd who fly in for the openings around town. From the menu she posts on her grid giving us a taste of what's in store, all I can gather that she's doing is that rich, white girl thing of arranging rather than actually getting her hands dirty and cooking. She says, *I have the best team around me, thank you so much for taking a chance on me, thank you to my loyal design team, you have no idea what we have in store.* I click through to all the people she tags and they are friends of her father—chefs, designers, critics and business owners of terrifyingly global brands backing her and seem to be providing the finance. How is she to run two businesses if the truth is, she doesn't actually run them at all? I watch her stake poles marking the plot of the café into the desert ground.

I want to gain immortality because of my brain and not because of the potential of my womb. I cast about for much of my life looking for a way in, inside myself. The desire to be an artist is something that burns inside of me all of my life but I can't get it out, I just don't know how to make anything, my hands are not skilled, they are as useful as two clay lumps. I don't have the patience to sit in the quiet. I want whatever it is to reveal itself to me now. I try dancing, drawing, sculpture, performance art, poetry. I am overwrought and sentimental. I am a lovesick teenager in tone and this does not make great art. Wanting to be an artist and being one are different. Perhaps I am just like everyone else and my disappointment is desiring to be special but not being special at all. Perhaps my life's purpose is to square myself with this. Toyin Ojih Odutola talks of our generation having to accept a hard truth that we may be the stepping stone to something greater in the future because it's not us. On a familial level, there are stories of Jim Carrey and Hanif Kureishi's fathers wanting to be writers and performers but not making it and of the guilt their children have to carry of their parent's unfulfilled dreams in tandem with their success. Maybe this is me. I am the fathers caught in an unchosen generation. I will have to learn how to amplify who comes next. I am the stepping stone because it is not me. I am mediocre. I have the will and desire but ultimately zero talent. I have to reconcile myself to being ordinary. I am like everybody else.

The man I want to be with makes things of extraordinary beauty. His mind is like a cathedral, where you would marvel awestruck at the ornate figures carved into the pillars, at the grace of the stained-glass Madonnas in the windows, at the light which spills through, the pain of it, that someone made all of this just for you is enough to move you to tears. Meeting him is like meeting the infinite, the point at which mystery is revealed. He is nothing I have ever encountered before. In our quieter, less fraught moments where I catch glimpses of what it could be between us, it is sharp and intense. He is the righteousness of exile, of reaching a momentary place of safety, of erecting cream coloured tents in the soil, the tautness of worshipping in defiance, the dewy breeze which brings the first exhale of spring banishing winter, haunting long-limbed trees draping over the small congregation, simple wooden symbols which bely a severity of worship, where the wood is more precious than gold, the priest wearing a small talisman on their lapel, everyone wearing the colour of bone, everyone, everyone, smiling serenely, this completely benign landscape and you, now belong to God.

a bump

OK but fr fr, what if all it is, is I am intoxicated with his money, the ease his money could provide any children I bring into the world. He is breathing access to the type of social mobility I want and can provide instant generational wealth. I could be threaded firmly into the backbone of Britain. If I have him then I don't need to try so hard on my own, I am saved from doing any real labour. Being with him is a hack for what I have to slog to achieve myself. He is collectively recognised as special and if other people see he sees me as special, I become special and other people will confer his specialness on to me.

I lay very still on my bed, my body heavy with hollow pressure. If I stay still then maybe I won't disturb the sadness which lodges itself between my organs, thickens my blood and keeps me tripping downwards into circular, repetitive thoughts. The mission to force the man I want to be with to see that he should be with me makes me weary. I am in a bad mood almost as soon as I wake up. I become difficult to be around. My friends shrink from me, unable to reach me, I am isolated, constantly checking my phone, moving rhythmically from his Instagram to hers many times a minute. I want to know what combination of words can break his silence—can his silence be broken. Telling him I love him and it being greeted with a cavernous void becomes addictive. These momentous words are greeted with blankness. It is appetising now, the taste of dead and deadness, the acrid dryness of forcing down bread I have burnt.

My mum is given a recommendation of a psychic called Kajal through her aqua aerobics class. She asks me if I want to see her to get some answers about the man I want to be with. I say yes. She texts her and they arrange an appointment for the following week in Portobello Market. When the day comes, I am nervous. This feels like witchy things that women do to ensnare men, but I want to ensnare him so here I am, I do the witchy things. We pass through the market, turn a corner and walk to the margins of the enclave where there is a white shed and a pathway opening to a car park. We enter the shed door. It is bright white inside with Mary figurines and small plaques dedicated to Jesus hanging on the walls. There are two plastic garden chairs in her makeshift reception, so we take both of them. A door opens in front of us and we see a young man and woman sitting in a shallow room. An older lady steps out and in a heavily accented voice says she will be free in a minute—her client is overrunning—and closes the door again. I am buzzing with energy, I don't know what will happen, will she tell me everything I want to hear.

A few minutes later, the door opens, the couple thank her, they both keep their eyes on the ground as they leave. Kajal beckons us in. There are no windows, only a small desk and four chairs which take up most of the room. Astrological charts and Ayurvedic diagrams in Hindi that I can't decipher are pinned to the walls. There are more figurines of Mary on the high shelves nearer the ceiling. She asks my mother to move her seat to the back of the room so as not to contaminate my reading. Kajal looks at me and I try to make her laugh because I am a clown and it is what I do when I am nervous. She asks me to put my right arm out on the table, inspects my palm and then flips my hand over. She asks me for my birth time and my mother answers, she asks what I am here for and I say, I want to find out if a man loves me. Kajal takes a piece of headed notepaper which has her name, a picture of an upturned hand, and her description as 'palmist, clairvoyant, crystal ball reader'. She writes the initials, A, M, S, P, J, H, D, R, K and says these initials are important to me. She tells me I did something bad to the man I want to be with in a past life and because of this I am paying for it now, there is stuck energy around me, I have a debt to pay and that is why he and I know each other now, he needs to make me suffer for this bad thing I did. She says there are snakes around me and she needs to break them. She says I will have two marriages in my life, the first one is not happy but the second one will be. She tells me the man I want to be with does love me but there are two women who surround him, one who is heavy in energy, who orders him about and makes him afraid and one where there is no love. She says, you will have two occupations at the same time. She tells me I will die in my bed when I am eighty-eight years old or over and it will be peaceful. She tells me I will go from being in the middle to being at the top of society. I take this as proof that the man I want to be with will be with me because he is at the top and being with him is how I will get there. Kajal tells me, you are like my daughter, I love you like a daughter. She turns to my mum and says, she's pretty, my mum beams. Kajal gives me an orange powder in a small plastic container and tells me to rub this on my face and put this in the corners of the house and my car. She tells me to put the powder on the man I want to be with's head and feet to break the dark energy around him. I cry and thank her and think this will make him be with me, this powder.

The man I want to be with is unpredictable. Every day I wake up thinking what it will be like with him today, will he be kind or cruel, will we speak today or will he ignore me, will the woman I am obsessed with take him away and ruin my life. Every week I ask my mother to text Kajal and beg her to tell me if the man I want to be with and I will be together, what we can do to make this happen, when will it happen, I need some guarantee. My mother wonders if we asked the wrong question, she says, we asked if he loved you not if he would be with you, but she does what I ask her, like she's a dealer. Kajal rings my mother after a few weeks and says we cannot contact her anymore, it's getting to be too much, she's done all she can for us and not to call her anymore.

light it up

I am furious as I prowl through the Paul Klee exhibition at Tate Modern with my boyfriend—I can't even say his name right, I say *kleeeee* instead of *clay* before I am corrected. Out of place, I whimper to my boyfriend, I don't understand this and he says, wait for them to come to you. I want to disrupt the smug complacency of the gallery. I shriek, I don't geddit into the echoey rooms and stomp around charging from painting to painting, breathing heavily, trying to make all the other people floating about anxious around me. I hate the beige walls and the reverence and the neatness and the abstract ideas I don't understand and the stupidity I feel towards all of the paintings stacked next to one another, decontextualised and really these are paintings about nothing—what arethese paintings of? It seems whimsical and twee and I hate that all of these white men could go to the Middle East or to countries in Africa, take from the cultures and steal the light and bring it back to the West and then somehow reinvent what was already there through the filter of the white imagination so that it is now Othered and distanced and beige-ified, so that their people could understand it all from some vantage of safety. Why do they take, why can't they give or just get out of the way? The fact that it is abstract makes me want to rip them from the walls, why do these paintings and the painter and the viewer get to look at an abstract portrayal of a world already abstracted for their convenience and comfort?

My boyfriend takes me to watch Pina Bausch's "1980" at Sadler's Wells. I don't understand it. I hiss at him that I want to walk out, I hate it, why did he bring me here, was it because he wanted to make me feel stupid, is that what it was, did he hate me, is this how he decides to tell me he thinks I'm an idiot. He keeps his eyes straight ahead and whispers my name to soothe me and shut me up. My lips twitch with how much I want to hurt him. He has brought me here to make me feel inferior. He turns his head towards me, his eyes glinting in the dark with worry and kindness. He had bought these tickets to expose me to new things, why was I being such an unlicensed bitch. He whispers, it's ok not to know what it is about, but to suspend my ego and watch. I tell him if he doesn't leave with me I will make him pay for it. He puts his hand on my arm and repeats he'd like to stay but if it is that unbearable, I should leave. Now he is telling me to leave! I furiously shake him off me, stand up in the dark, disturb all the people in my row and I leave feeling liberated. I have acted independently, I have rebelled, stood up for good taste by walking out. When I am back in our flat, I lay on our bed, seething. I can tell he is apprehensive from the way he unlocks the front door. I am completely cold and refuse to look at him but once he cajoles me into talking, I leap on him and we have a claustrophobic fight. I am grappling with ideas I can't articulate, feeling like he has betrayed me in some way.

My boyfriend buys me tickets to a play, so we cycle from our flat to Sadler's Wells, buy drinks at the bar and order our interval drinks. They call for our row to come forward and we hand our tickets to the usher. The usher looks confused and says, these are for the Barbican. By this time it is almost too late to make it but we try. We rush out to our bikes and attempt to cycle down in ten minutes, which is impossible. I am fuming at his stupidity in not checking the tickets, how the fuck did he get the Barbican and Sadler's Wells confused? Why would he cause me this unnecessary pain? Once we arrive at the Barbican, they tell us we can't come in until the interval and really by then it's too late. Under the Brutalist architecture and surrounded by water, greenery and the concrete that feels like home to me—I scream at him. I scream at him and call him a fucking cunt for getting it wrong, he wasted money, we missed the show, I scream until my hair turns into a basket of snakes not caring if there are residents looking out of windows or of the genteel people walking to shows and drinks and dates, averting their eyes from this unhappy couple having a meltdown in public. My boyfriend tries to escape from my verbal onslaught but I hunt him down through the maze of buildings swearing at him, spitting contempt out in poisonous bloody bites, him in a brace position and only when I get tired do we go home. I behave like this with him in public. I intentionally belittle him in front of our friends, or else I try to make out as if I am not with him when we are with people we don't know, I want him to leave or leave me alone. When we are at home together it is different. Most of the time I am needy and affectionate but when we are in public I am made of stone. We have fights that come from nowhere. I lose control of myself and we come up with the coping strategy of my leaving our tiny flat—sometimes at two in the morning— to cool off my rage because if I stay inside, I will hit him. And I don't mean Hollywood lady smacks. I want to tear the flat apart. I belt him with my open hands, or to provide an even better blow, not exactly punch, but thump my fists down on his back and sides. He pins me down on the bed to stop me hitting him whilst I thrash about violently trying to throw him off me and he will breathe slowly to soften me until I cry with remorse, his blue eyes holding me together so I'm not fully aware of how much I hurt him. I vacate my mind when these episodes occur. There is a dragon which consumes me, breathing fire, burning everything and all of him into a crisp. I am a pit of self-loathing. He plunges care and love into me but it only makes me hate him even more. Both of us pretend this part of our relationship is a bad dream.

I am used to presenting myself as one thing but doing what
I want in secret. I am used to changing my clothes to go to day-timers
like Pop Ya Cherry in Harrow Leisure Centre or at Equinox in Leicester
Square where I went as a teenager but is now long closed. The bouncers
would turn a blind eye and let us in with our dodgily made ID where
we were suddenly morphed into a middle-aged EU student. It was here
I had my first kiss, by which I mean I stuck my tongue out and hoped
for the best because I just wanted to be kissed, I just wanted something
adult to happen to me. I am used to changing back into normal clothes
again so I could be home before dinner with no one any the wiser. I am
used to sex being out of reach, something out there, not regular but the
only site of rebellion available to me because my parents didn't want
me to do it, so I obviously end up wanting to do it in order to have some
bodily autonomy. I am used to secrets, the illicitness, the addictive
quality to them, to knowing more than everyone around me, the
power I could gain in a situation and the resentment which builds up
against your authority figures for being so stupid, how can they not
know of the Trojan Horse-like plans you make but instead of Troy,
you're invading some shit club in Wembley. I am used to wondering if
I am good enough. I am used to hiding parts of myself from my
parents, and then hiding parts of myself from my friends, and hiding
parts of myself from boys I liked, and hiding parts of myself from the
society I belonged to that didn't like the brown bits of me, and then
hiding parts of myself from my family who didn't like the parts of me
that loved drugs and techno and staying out all night and sex and
cocks and cunts and come and booze and freedom. I am used to living

inside of shame, I am used to being on the outside breathing mist up on the glass begging to be let in. I am absolutely primed for this affair. It is toxic and familiar.

hawk

After our fights, I do not remember any of the things I say to my boyfriend, all I know is that I am hateful in the moment, a whirling dervish of lashes. He needs days to recover because the things I say to him hurt so much and he remembers it all. We are more tender with each other after these fights, quieter as he recovers. I will stroke his forehead and kiss the sides of his nose, I'll bite the back of his upper arms which make my mouth water. I wonder if he tolerates the fights because, in my remorse, I am gentle with him. I wait for him to come back to me.

My mother and I sit opposite one another on the stairs. We find we can talk here without my dad listening in, though he finds an excuse to walk past to eavesdrop on what we're saying. When we're in the living room he will watch us from the door. We've caught him pausing to listen through the crack when one of us has unexpectedly flung the door open. Here on the stairs, we have a bird's eye view and can swiftly change the subject when he appears, side-eyeing us as he walks past, moving round the house with no real motivation to do so. I tell my mum I'm cheating on my boyfriend with the man I want to be with. I tell her the sex is good even though we don't seem to have it anymore and I tell her about the cathedral vistas I feel with him. She says, I told you not to be with your boyfriend, I said keep him as a friend. I snap, that doesn't help me much now. My dad walks past and my mother segues smoothly into talking about my cousins. He walks past again and I nod in agreement and say, well you know, you never could trust them and she says, yeah I don't know why they keep doing this. Once he's clear my mother says, you don't want to end up like me. I couldn't live without your dad but I'm not in love with him. We hear a door bang and we know he's gone out into the garden so we have a few minutes. She tells me, when I look at you and your boyfriend, I see your dad and me, it'll be safe but it'll be stale. I say, so you're friends, and she says, yeah, we're friends. I tell her how proud I am of walking in public with the man I want to be with, how I want to be seen with him, it's a kind of pride I don't have with my boyfriend where we always stay in. She looks at me and nods and I realise that although she is a homebody, this lack of pride might also be a reason why she doesn't like going out. My dad isn't someone to show off, won't make other women jealous, so why be seen in public. I tell her, we don't sleep together, my boyfriend and I, we don't have sex. I feel like an old person, sex is something other people have not me. I hear my dad opening the shed door, the creaks sound like all the tension in my body. I look back at my mum. She says, I'll support you if you want to leave him. She keeps her black eyes on my face to gauge my reaction and says, you can come back home.

eight sides

The woman I am obsessed with likes to convey she has a deeper, more nuanced understanding of things like hospitality, food, nature, words and art. I want to say to her, so you have nothing but white innocence because you are not aware of the inherent violence of your hospitality, your food, your concepts of nature, your words, why do I have to carry the burden of history. She is free to believe it is all in the past and no one ever interrogates her because they have the same mindset too. It's a veritable feedback loop, all of them back-patting their own outlooks.

She ardently believes she has a symbiotic relationship with poetry, with the magic in constructing sentences. Her father's success means she sees it as ordained by blood. She believes his MacArthur award is a joint effort won by them both. She says people think she too shares his gift, and this is confirmed by her many fans who gushingly thank her for her words when she picks up and puts down whatever flavour-of-the-week social justice cause she decides to write a caption about. She takes night walks, has her run at national nature reserves in the middle of a weekday using hashtags like #selfcare as if she is the burnt-out CEO of a conglomerate. She photographs shadows and sunsets and art from the fifties and wants us, her fans, to know that she has some twelfth artistic sense which we are given access to—she actually is so generous sharing her privileged education with us and we should be grateful. Annoyingly, I learn about art history and artists from her. Through her mini Insta-lessons, I develop my own tastes in contemporary art and I position myself against her overly educated cerebral language. My knowledge is centred around my bodily responses so I can ground myself with authority and hide all the theory I just do not know.

on a downward spiral

Why do I know all this? My mind is full of junk about her but I can't stop needing to find out more. I ask the man I want to be with how he could put up with her because anything I read or listen to of hers makes my eyes roll to the back of my head, it's so easily puncturable. He says, you should really stop looking her up and then says, he would poke fun at her but she couldn't laugh at herself and he tried his best to soften her, to change her and she was different when he had her on her own. He says he was cunt struck.

knees

I make the long drive back to London as I have arranged to meet the man I want to be with in the evening. I have energy for him in a way I don't have for my boyfriend. It is a week before Christmas. We meet in Soho, I wear skin-tight clothes, a black top which plunges down to my navel. When I stand to order another drink, a table full of men stop talking and stare at me at the bar and then their eyes swivel to look at him, assessing us together. When I sit down, I laugh and say, did you see that? He says, did you? And I say, of course I did. We walk to the station. I put my hand in my pocket to text my boyfriend I am coming home and then put my phone away again. We say goodbye at the bottom of the escalator at Tottenham Court Road and the man I want to be with disappears northbound and I head south. I put my hand in my pocket again but my phone isn't there anymore. I sweat from every pore in my body. I need my phone for work, it's basically where I do my job from, how do I get home, how do I do the long drive back to work without it? I walk the entire length of Oxford Street looking hopelessly at the ground for it to turn up somehow and then I walk back up again with my eyes frantically sweeping the roads and the pavement. It is nowhere.

When I am home, I tell my boyfriend I have been pick-pocketed and he is in a muddle for me. He digs out an old iPhone of his and lets me borrow it. From my laptop I email the man I want to be with telling him to give me his number again as I have lost my phone. I write down my mum's number, my boyfriend's and the man I want to be with's number on a piece of paper as emergency numbers. The next day I visit my mother. I tell my boyfriend I am staying late to see my cousins and instead I arrange to meet the man I want to be with using the borrowed iPhone. The man I want to be with texts to confirm the details and I reply and say, yes that's great. I am waiting impatiently at home for the time to pass so I can leave and be with him. I am always early so I try to be late but more often than not I'm there before him. My boyfriend calls and I answer and say hey and use the nickname we have for one another. He is quiet and then he says, I know. Perplexed, I ask, know what, and he replies, I know what you're doing, where you're going. My eyes widen. My mum looks at me intently and I mouth, oh my god, he knows. Her eyes bulge. You know what, I say and he says, I know who you're meeting. I ask how and he says, Apple keeps everything linked so that phone you're using is connected to my phone so I've seen your messages. He asks, what are you going to do and I say defiantly, I am still going, I'll see you at home and hang up.

I do not tell the man I want to be with that my boyfriend has found out, it roots too much to reality and I want to stay in the dream. When I return to the flat, I am steely. I tell my boyfriend, yes ok I am attracted to him but the man I want to be with has no idea, it's me who has got carried away. I think I am being valiant. I leave for work early in the morning. I am supposed to be away for a week. Later in the day, my boyfriend texts me to tell me he is coming to visit me. I am staying with his mother in a city about two hours away so he has every right to come and see us but I see it as an invasion. We don't talk until we go to bed and I am irritated I have to share my bed with him and he says, if you had never worked away you would never have got used to being alone. He pauses and asks, so what do you want to do and painfully I lurch forward with the power he gives me. Months later, it's a moment he cannot forgive himself for—the way he gave himself away for so little. I realise there is nothing I can do that will make him break up with me. He should have been throwing me out but he doesn't. In his small way he begs, and I know what it means to beg.

I'll probably be accused of leveraging this relationship to get the status I want but if I can't get it from having him, I'll get it from telling you how I couldn't.

i'll huff and i'll puff

As a teenager, I needed to be an ogre at home to frighten my parents so they didn't frighten me. If I breathed fire against them then I would scorch the earth around me to have some semblance of autonomy. I amplified my rage to protect myself but then it was like I stretched my belly and no amount of rage was ever enough. If I made them frightened of me, they wouldn't ask me where I was going and I could do what I wanted without their fear of what the community would think. This abstract idea of 'community' was enough of a reason to police my behaviour, my body and my actions.

weeds

My boyfriend and I spend the last week we have in the flat separating our belongings. Neither of us can bear to start earlier than this as the flat is the closest thing we have to a child and the process of taking our shared life apart is like splitting a carcass, the blade working its way through bone. We divide up the books, put our beloved purple sofa and our two huge bookcases up on Freecycle where a man comes with a van to collect them and we're sure he'll sell them, not use them himself as is the spirit of the forum but we let it go without a fight. We give away our two bedside drawers which were given to us by a woman who said they had served her family home for ten years and she hoped they might bring us happiness as they had brought her and her home happiness. We clean the flat and we do this together. We scrape the orange mould from the bathroom tiles, we wash the shower curtain we bought to replace the one that came with the flat because the mould had ruined it so thoroughly, we clean the grout in the windows, we wipe the top of the skirting board, I finally clear five years' worth of my tax envelopes I haven't ever opened and we drive to the recycling centre together, filling up my car in three round trips to get rid of the things neither of us can use or give away. The final night before we leave, I ask to stay over and we lay beside one another but don't touch and in his sleep my boyfriend's face looks pinched, pale and drawn. I don't clean the top of the cooker hood properly, I leave a smear, so the agent asks for a receipt to prove we used a professional cleaning company and when we say we did the job ourselves, they take my boyfriend's entire deposit and he is angry with me. A man wearing a very neat suit comes over to take the photos that will end up proving the need to keep the deposit and asks where we're moving to, and we pause unsure if the other will tell the truth. When the silence continues for just a bit too long, a frown starts to flicker on the estate agent's face and my boyfriend eventually speaks up and says, we're not sure yet.

On our last trip down to the car, our downstairs neighbour who has an amiable way about him but only talks to my boyfriend and not to me, asks where we're going, and we both pause again unable to tell this stranger we have failed. My boyfriend finally says, oh we're having a clear-out and the neighbour looks at both of us, narrowing his eyes to assess if this is true, sensing something isn't right but then abruptly says, ok, see you later, and heads upstairs. We put the final boxes in my car, take the last of his things to the storage space down the road as he's sure he'll be back in London but it will turn out he never comes back. We are more courteous and more generous with each other, but we are quiet. I give him a lift to Elephant and Castle where he wants to pick up some weed from his dealer before going to his mum's. Neither of us are able to say goodbye and when he eventually says, right, and opens the door to get his bags, he mouths I love you as he walks on the pavement and I pull away, tears obscuring everything.

you're on your own kid

I come back home almost exactly the way I left it, my punt at rebellion quashed quite spectacularly. It is a humiliating homecoming and I have nothing to show for ten years of working, almost no financial solvency. The relationship with my family is so fraught that it is traumatic to share the same living space with them again. Years and years of resentment and grudges and misunderstandings roll like thunder under the carpet, the rain soaks the walls in the living room, the water saturates the ceiling. Three nights after I move back in, my brother tears through the house and we have a screaming match bringing up old grudges from when he was thirteen. A cousin texts and says, I think you made a mistake you should stay with your boyfriend, the implication being, you're too old to be single. Two of our closest friends stop talking to me for a year because the end of the relationship means the end of heartbreak hotel.

When I tell the man I want to be with that I've broken up with my boyfriend he texts back, I hope you didn't do this because of me. A week after I move back home, we meet in a pub in Bow. I am hyper and fraught but I think I'm being normal and sexy. He breaks his one kiss per meeting rule and kisses me spontaneously inside the pub and says afterwards, I kissed you so you would calm down—you were spiralling. I go to the toilet thinking he'll be watching me as I walk away, completely enthralled by me. I glance back and he's looking at his phone. When I'm in the cubicle, I do not go for a wee. I keep my trousers up. I stand and do nothing, upright in the too narrow cubicle like I'm standing in my own grave. I walk to the sinks and look at my reflection in the mirror. I stare at my face mutated under the spotlights my features morphing into the mask of a hysteric. My eyes are barely contained panic in a tense face. I am waiting for the man I want to be with to tell me he will be with me. I am down like a runner poised for the sound of the starting gun and then I will run and run and run and run and run. Someone walks in and it startles me. I pretend I've finished washing my hands and put them under the dryer. I am performing all the time, performing being myself, what is myself, who is me. I step back out into the pub and he is still on his phone like the bored receptionist at the mouth of hell. I stand next to him so he will notice me. He doesn't and I keep standing, waiting for a command which doesn't come.

bite me

I wonder what it's like to have women buzzing around him, crying, or angry, or sending him nudes to entice him back to them or playing it cool because some of them have just started and everyone is at different emotional registers and in different time zones. Eliciting all that female attention and desire at once must be addictive. He must have felt quite good, looking at his phone in the morning. It leads me to believe with dizzying certainty that when there is a man involved, and a rich one at that—especially with a dick like his—there is no such thing as a sisterhood. It's every female for herself.

if i was a worm would you still love me

Society told me, anything a man can do I can do, but it turns out it is not true. Our experience of time is markedly different. What they say about women having a shelf life, everything they said was true, all the women who I scorned for inhaling the patriarchal ideas of a sell-by date, the 'ripeness' of women, the 'freshness', my mother who told me to pick carefully, they were right and now I have to make a concerted effort to stem the tsunami of fear at being imprisoned by my gender—which now means not having any control over the meaning of myself. The man I want to be with is at an age where he should know better what he wants, but he doesn't need to. The fact of his being a man means he is coddled. The world does not demand any self-awareness from him. He has the ability to say to me he needs time to decide which way his life will go— he can still say he might want children at an age where for a woman this would be impossible. The fact he can say this says everything about the power he holds versus the power my fertility has over me, the upper hand men have over women, because although women experience the infinite, our value is not seen as infinite, our value is tied to our small window of production and it is a daily effort to fight the fear we have no value outside the parameters of marriage and children, if it is possible to do this at all. Capitalism stokes the illusion the planet's resources are never-ending or else that things only have value when they are producing and if they are not, then replace them. Plants, business, creativity, sexuality, nature, women, fear, envy, outrage must be in constant supply to sustain a false premise of growth, progress or profit. Men are perceived as steady, reliable capitalistic servants. They are almost machines, able to reproduce at any age, three hundred and sixty-five days of the year. Men's bodies are a part of the workforce their whole lives as they never need breaks for menstruation, maternity or menopause. Men's time is believed to be limitless. There is no shelf life for the man I want to be with like there is for me, there is no cliff face, he can be forever perusing. I have to have had a whole life before I am thirty, will be deemed old at thirty-five, yet he has the ability to remake his life at whatever age he wants, the possibility of starting afresh with a younger face is always open to him. He wastes women's time, which to me is the most heinous crime he commits and the second is his lack of remorse. The validation a relationship bestows upon a woman's personhood still exists and has to be internally fought off if a union hasn't been achieved. The world is built for couples. Even unhappy ones.

The man I want to be with is Daddy in his working life which he populates with men but is Baby in his intimate relationships with women. I think we all went in expecting something rather different to what we ended up with. We wanted a man but ended up with a dependent. Meeting up is restricted to lunchtimes only, lest he be accused of being on a date and in the evenings he will implement a communication blackout from six in the evening and then will text me again from half ten or eleven from his sofa once his wife goes to bed, or he will text garbled monosyllabic messages when she goes to the loo to which I text back, ?

I think, though he completely ignores any public mention of his wife, in private he tells her he needs her and that he doesn't need to openly declare this fact if he already spends his life with her. I could confidently guess he is the little spoon, or that she is the one to put her arm around him and he will sit like a cat in her lap. He tells me he has no desire for her and I think he will leave her because he is so often hard around me. But he leaves out that he enjoys her care, his flat, and that really sex isn't that important to him, which means he won't be leaving even though he says he might one day. He loves magic, loves the deception, the concealment and the secrecy and is expert at it, and dabbles in a kind of conceptual treasure hunt. He has such power with his words, with the images he creates. You truly feel like you are sharing a life with him just because he dreamed it so. It's only when you are apart that you realise you are apart because the relationship is not real but by then he's onto the next thing and the next person and you are something far away again. You have to maintain the illusion all by yourself and like a surveyor, he may come back to check it's all still running the way he left it but he won't do the heavy-lifting.

Once words become hollowed out and untrustworthy, resentment sets in. I put him down in our conversations and call him stupid, I am self-righteous and brittle and over the course of our whatever-ship, really I wish something bad would happen to him. Not death exactly, but near enough that he realises it's me he should be with. Unfortunately, he stays well even though he doesn't drink water and he eats pizza and fish and chips all the time. One day when I'm sitting in traffic over that beautiful bridge in Chelsea, he texts me to tell me he's suffering from a mystery pain and is at the doctors and updates me with how he gets on through his day, tells me like the way you would a girlfriend, check in and update them. I am flattered and worried. I inexplicably start to heave with sobs because it hits me that, if he did get sick, no one would know who I am to him, he'd be rushed to the hospital and the nurses would say, *only family at this time* and no one would call me, not a mutual friend because we have none and people in his circle do not connect us the way the woman I am obsessed with is connected to him, they wouldn't say to me, *the man you want to be with is in the hospital, don't worry he's fine but he's asked for you*, I wouldn't be able to do a dramatic, drop everything, my boyfriend is *sick!* and rush to his side with no make-up on but moisturised, in a tank and culottes and my birks, where you can see I'm pretty but I haven't made an effort, *I'm tired* and *stressed, my lover* is in the *hospital!* and I sit there with his hand in my hand watching over him like I'm a fucking saint, brushing his beautiful hair off his face and he opens his eyes and I'm like, hey you, and he says, it's you, I made a mistake. I won't get that moment. Instead I cry alone in the car and text him and say, if you got sick who would tell me, I'm crying and he panics and says, I would tell you, please stop crying. I say, what if you were so sick you couldn't tell me, then what? I'm nothing to you, I don't even know what I am to you, and over text he clucks and soothes and I'm hiccupping in the car and he says, you're crazy, but gently and affectionately and I feel like those kooky girls in romcoms who have these storms of emotion all the time and he is like the stalwart boyfriend, like, *this woman is a mystery to me!* Except I'm not anything to him and nothing to myself which is why I stay, and he enjoys all of us, gets something whole out of a multitude of people and I put up with it because a bit of him is better than nothing at all.

unbothered moisturised happy
in my lane focused flourishing

We have our first fight outside the Half Moon in Herne Hill in the street. We have been walking for fifteen minutes, arms wrapped around each other, not looking where we are going, kissing like we are lapping cream. It is very teenage—more so because I had never done this as a teenager. We have nowhere to go indoors, both our partners like parental figures forbidding sex inside the house, but we have the street and we kiss there. He tells me the woman I am obsessed with is coming to London next month. This is before I know her name, three months after he's put the blanket ban on sex with me. She is travelling but will make a pit stop in London to visit her half-sister and while she is here, he will meet her. I let go of him and keep walking in a daze like I've been struck, the cream on my tongue instantly sours. I've not ever felt my heart do the things it's doing. I've never felt the physical limits of my heart before. How can it hurt this much? He looks off longingly into the distance and says, she was so anxious at the prospect of seeing me last time that she threw up and couldn't leave her hotel room, we didn't even see each other. There flashes a secret wonderment in his face at having this effect on her. He says, if she flies into the country, I will see her. I ask, why? it's over, why do you need to see her? He says with pain slashed across his features, if she wants to see me, I will see her, I'm not sure if we'll sleep together but she still has a hold on me and I don't even know why, I'm not even into white girls.

I stare across at Brockwell Park. I am on home turf, kissing a man who isn't my boyfriend who I wish was my boyfriend and he is wishing he was kissing someone else who he doesn't want to make his girlfriend.

My voice cracks and I say, what about me? You have a hold on me. He finally brings his attention back to me but I take off, hoping he'll follow me with some sort of declaration but he doesn't, he walks to the bus stop and waits to be taken home.

the other side

      My mother finds another psychic, another recommendation she gets from her aqua aerobics class, a woman called Kiera. She does sessions over WhatsApp. My mother doesn't consult me before contacting her, she messages her and pays for a session and tells me when it is. My mum has tried to do it without me but Kiera told her it's difficult without me being present. I am angry with my mother. I tell her she needs to seek my consent before she does this, poking around in my future. I take the appointment. Kiera asks for a photo of me before our session. At the time allocated, she messages and welcomes me. She tells me the spirit of an older woman, who is small and has her hair in a bun, watches over me, I say, this is my grandmother on my mum's side who is dead. Kiera says, she is gentle and says I did the right thing concerning a health complication and to move forward with it. She tells me children are going to come quickly for me, she sees the month of March. She tells me there are two moves that she can see around the home, one on my own and the second is with someone else and it is settled and romantic, it will be with someone with fresh energy. I ask to send a photo of the man I want to be with, I want to know if it is him she is talking about. I submit a photo I find online of him and she says, she has an uneasy feeling around him, blockages, his energy is confusing and he is not truthful in his feelings. She says, he's not to be trusted and I keep hearing 'the grass isn't greener on the other side'. She says, he has push/pull energy, it makes me feel frustrated for you, do not wrap your energy here with him or waste time here, he wants to have his cake and eat it too. I can see you trying to hold things together and trying to keep an active reason for the decisions that you have made but you must be able to let go here. She tells me he is a stepping stone to get me out of my relationship. She tells me things about my writing and my work. I find it hard to believe her when she says there is no future here with him when I can see it so fervently. She pulls tarot cards for me but by then I have decided she is a hack. Once she signs off, I text the man I want to be with and ask him when he's free to meet.

dumb

The man I want to be with is one of the cleverest people I've ever met and this is part of the reason I am so intrigued by him. When it comes to emotions, emoting or verbalising emotions however, he is frozen, he blocks and he evades. I am patient at first because I do not know the kind of intractability I am up against but even when it hits me he won't change, I dogmatically believe he will. When he tells me he can't be with me, I am indignant. I am consecrated. I am made holy, beyond reproach. I punish him with my emotional fluency. I enjoy making him feel stupid, I enjoy his panic, I enjoy the blank look on his face. I enjoy the curl of my lip in contempt of his complete bafflement at how to be a human being on earth, he seems zapped here by aliens, dancing lightly on the surface of life, antithetical to love. I enjoy his abject fear at my attempts to root him to the ground. I enjoy assuming I know more about his emotional landscape than he does and making grand proclamations like a Poundland Cassandra. I enjoy rolling my eyes at him and saying, you're the stupidest cleverest person I've ever known, I enjoy telling him I don't know how he's got through life tricking people into thinking he's smart, I enjoy telling him he's thick. I enjoy behaving like his therapist because it means I have power and a secret knowledge that puts me slightly above him. I enjoy his deference to me when I talk seemingly authoritatively about race as if I know how the world really works because it makes me seem more important than I actually am. When I feel like I'm losing the argument I can say witheringly, you just don't understand, which shuts him up and covers for the fact that I'm not sure how things are either. He is deliberately obstructive when I press him to talk about his inner world. I don't understand how he can be such a mystery to himself, both believing he is not important enough to occupy himself with women and too important to think about relationships. When he hurts me (un)intentionally by telling the truth or not enough of it, by doing too much one way and not another, I enjoy telling him he's a cunt and a bastard and I hate him and he's evil. I scream, he's a misogynist, he hates women, I see it as a quagmire at the centre of him and he says, yes, I do, I hate women. I blame his mother. I say your mother is unable to praise you and so you seek the adoration of women around you. He agrees with me. He enjoys hearing my insults hurled at him like Molotov cocktails, almost closing his eyes in ecstasy.

normalise saying, for a yt person, after complimenting yt people

The woman I am obsessed with lives in a state of suspended teenagedom or early retirement. She takes photos of the plants she finds on her walks and labels them with their scientific Latin names like it means something in her stories as if the point of these walks is to educate in this way and not because she has countless hours to fill. She likes to classify art, plants and art history and explain them to her fans. Her fans who are primarily white too, enjoy her cutting up and labelling the world as she finds it. She has said people have found her Instagram a peaceful place to be, a salve to the chaos of the world. She spotlights artists on Terroir's Instagram, and although she doesn't work with any Black, female-identifying or non-Black minority artists, as in pay them, she uses their faces to adorn her grid to give the illusion of someone who is concerned about representation (I have often written furious comments pulling her up about this under her posts and then deleted them straightaway). She inserts herself into the narrative as if she needs to be there to make sense of it for you. The Othered image or object or person needs to be processed through her eyes, her brain and then her fingers, transformed into captions on Instagram, which then turbo charge its value. In this way, she signals her approval, which then leads to other white people paying attention to it and then admitting it into their personal canons.

This is whiteness. It is everywhere, pervasive, its assumption that it needs to be there to sanitise, to give order by creating a hierarchy. Whiteness on its own is empty, it is forceful in its insistence of its peculiar quality of absence. It refuses to be described in and of itself and instead it needs some other thing to define itself against. In whiteness' view everything else is full of itself, so full and busy with living that those things cannot have the panoramic view which only whiteness can offer. Whiteness is nihilistic, it is the distilled form of the death drive and because it has a cold separation to life, it believes it alone is able to categorise, is the one to get rid of the excess, the one to do the accounts, to formulate the systems that regulate the chaos, to decide who lives or dies—it alone can shoulder this responsibility it made up for itself, so anxiously adrift it is without a purpose. Time must remain static so whiteness' power can be maintained by any means. The object, the story, the person or the plant cannot follow its own orbit or rhythmic evolution because whiteness forces it into subjugation. Whiteness and white people make themselves pervasive yet think of themselves as separate. It is parental and condescending in tone—it invented the concept of race conferring upon itself—a freak genetic accident—the values of intelligence, advancement, beauty, whereby the lower the level of melanin in the body, the higher your place in the hierarchy, the lighter the skin tone, the closer you are to whiteness therefore the better, more beautiful you are regarded, the more suited to power you are. The simplicity of this belief is in tandem with its terrible violence. Whiteness believes that all things need an organising principle and by chance it has the answer—the principle it offers is itself.

tourist

My parents go on a package holiday to India with a crowd of white British people. One of their Indian tour guides stands next to my dad and puzzled asks him what he's doing here with these people, doesn't he have family to stay with. My mum collects the numbers of people called Shirley and Helen and for a few weeks after they come back, she spends hours on the phone talking to these white women. My parents say wistfully it's the best holiday they have ever been on. There's a photo of the two of them with about twenty indistinguishable white blobs outside the Taj Mahal, all with their arms open, all wearing those awful boomer shades screaming happily into the camera.

I'm at Blenheim Palace for work with about two hundred people around me. I'm trading fast emails with the man I want to be with. We've not been talking long at this point but I am too eager and available, I answer him straightaway and then have to wait for his replies. My life isn't busy enough for me to be sexy and I don't know what it is to play hard to get. He asks me if I've ever seen *Naked Attraction* and I say no. He says it's very interesting seeing peoples' naked bodies. The flatness descends. I say I've never watched it. He pings back, do you draw? And I say, I do a bit but I don't think I'm very good. He replies, one day we should draw each other naked, what do you think about that? When I read this, it is like I wake up from a deep, deep sleep. I am immediately awake, it's as if my eyes are open for the first time. It is the moment my life begins. I say, ok but I have really hairy legs I'm trying to get comfortable with the hair on my legs, and he says, I don't mind about the hair on your body, I really like drawing hair, it's meditative. He offers somewhere comfortable like a hotel room and when I reply I screw my nose up in distaste, if it's to draw one another then there can't be a bed in the room, what about a dance studio. He says, it has to be warm. I can find somewhere, I reply, wondering, is he flirting with me, I can't tell. I don't hear anything back for the rest of the day. I am heartsick. I go home to my boyfriend clinging to my phone. The man I want to be with emails three days later and says something has come up at home and so our plans will have to be put on hold, perhaps you will be glad to hear this, I'll be in touch. We don't speak again for seven months.

as a treat

Mocha and I are friends. He looks at me with love now, I can tell. Leah gives me his favourite biscuits and I sneak them to him in the park. I see Djuna in the distance with Milo, she's wearing one of the navy-blue jumpsuits sold by the woman I am obsessed with. The fabric looks expensive even from this distance. I call out, come on Mocha, and he bounds up and down wagging his tail looking up at me with his tongue hanging out. I think this is how I love the man I want to be with, doing what he says for the remote promise of treats and being tolerated because of how much I love him. I bend down, unclip the dog's leash, stroke his head and start running and hopping to get him excited and he starts doing turns and yapping with happiness. I try and pretend to be unaware of Djuna as I approach them, totally focused on the dog but I can see my movement and the dog makes them both look up and inside I punch my fist. My phone starts ringing, it's a number I don't recognise so I assume it's a work call. I stop a little way off from them to answer it. As I'm talking to the person on the phone, I watch Mocha wander off, smelling the edges of the grass on the path and sniffing around trees. Milo starts making her way over, clasping her hands, her eyes shimmering. Mocha doesn't notice her and carries on sniffing and wandering in their direction. Djuna has her eyes on her child and the dog. I half turn and keep the call going by asking inane questions I don't need the answer to. Milo comes up close to Mocha and hugs him and Mocha is surprised but gently submits to the adoration. Milo shouts, mummy mummy, and Djuna walks over to them. I abruptly end the call and I walk towards them saying, oh my god I'm so sorry I got distracted by the phone, and she says, no it's fine she likes dogs. Djuna has the kind of beautiful lines on her face which tell you she was an extraordinarily beautiful young person and carries herself that way as an extraordinarily beautiful slightly older person. She has clear eyes, is tall, her outfit lends her that kind of actress off-duty carelessness, revelling in being a bit low-key. She says your dog is so sweet and I say, he loves kids. Mocha and Milo are playing chase. I reach towards her almost touching the edge of the fabric of the jumpsuit and say, I love this it's stunning, so well made and she looks down at it as if seeing it for the first time and says, oh thanks, but says no more. They're becoming good friends, I say, nodding at Mocha and Milo, I hate to tear them apart and she replies, she just loves animals. I let her watch them for a little while, saying nothing. She seems like a good mother. A good wife. I can't blow this. I have to let her come to me. She turns to me and asks, do you live locally and I nod and give Leah's address as my rough location and she exclaims, that's super close! I say this park is one of my faves and she says, yes, it's a good one. I don't know if mentioning I know who she is or not is better, which one turns me into a fan and which one makes me her equal. I look at her body and think, you have been in close proximity to the woman I am obsessed with, the same blood which runs in her, runs in you. I say, ah I probably have to be off and call out to Mocha. Milo emits an awwwwwwwww and then as the dog comes to me, Milo starts crying. I'll be good with her child and that'll show her I am harmless. I say, that's ok we can see you again, I say it's not goodbye, it's see you later. She whimpers, see you later, with tears dripping onto Mocha's head and Mocha nuzzles the girl and as I am on the ground with my arms around them both, I look up at Djuna and say, oh my god this is too cute, and Djuna throws her head back and she laughs.

The woman I am obsessed with moves to her own place in Marfa. I am not sure if she's bought it with her huge advance from the book she's written or if she's renting. I want to know if she receives a personal income.

I suddenly become obsessed with owning my own home and want to know what I'd have to do to get one. I get the number of a mortgage broker off a friend and my dad takes over the contact, speaking to the broker about how he and my mum would have to reorganise their finances in order for me to be a homeowner. It all hinges on the regularity of my work and if I am able to pay the bills, but due to the precariousness of my income this is thrown out of balance. I've got in my own way again and wish I could have another go at life where I had a more regular wage and was less concerned about expressing myself, which doesn't pay the bills. My mum tells me the broker is my age. The broker says my dad reminds her of hers and she wants to look after him, get him the best deal. The frequent phone calls my dad and the broker have about getting me a mortgage go dead when it turns out we'd have to prove to the bank I could pay the mortgage. It dies with one call I have with her where I laugh hysterically at my own jokes and take the piss out of the process as if I'm too cool to have a regular job, I have a cool person's job where everything is insecure and seasonal, like I was too busy being cool and sexy to figure out tax brackets, my god. She says worriedly, will you get a job and can you get one for three months at least, will you be able to make these regular payments? I say, I'm sure I will but I get jobs via word of mouth so it'll come I'm just not certain when. She goes silent and then tells me, if I can't pay the mortgage for whatever reason, she'll put a clause in the agreement that they can't come for my parents' house and that I could rent the flat out if I found myself unable to pay. I say, sounds like a good plan. I try to make her like me, as if she's someone I've met at a bar. I am not sure why I do this. I don't like the power she has in her potential judgement of my lack of secure life choices. She resists my tempting her to take a more informal route to our conversation as if I could charm her into turning around and saying *hey I like you, you can have a house!* I can hear how unsure she is of my abilities as an adult and how serious I am as a person on the other end of the phone. I sound like a manic teenager. I wonder how the man I want to be with's finances are organised. I know he supports his wife, that she doesn't need to work, that she is able to pursue her creativity far beyond the point where others would have had to give up.

I attack his wife to hurt him. I have seen some of her collages and I see no life in them. They are like a shitty A Level project but I am unjustly judging her in their place. He asks me over text, what is it with women and taking ages to get ready, and I spit back, what the fuck would you know about how long it takes for a woman to get ready, it doesn't seem like your wife looks too long in the mirror. I feel a sick, delighted thrill at abusing her when she can't defend herself. I show my hand and reveal I have been stalking her and I know what she looks like, even though there is scant evidence of her online. I tell him, you finance her art, she's never had to do anything else and yet she still can't make an impact, so she must be shit. She should have been the country's best artist, what the fuck else was in her way. He says nothing. I used to think his lack of defence for her was because he agreed with me but now I know his silence is there because he is loyal to her but chooses the path of least resistance with me and in the gap I make up my own meaning, which is that he loves me more. I am jealous he covers all of their bills. I want to be with him so he can take care of my bills. Although emotionally he is a child, he is a provider. I wonder if she does the admin because he insists on staying in the fantasy land of his imagination or if he does the admin because he wants to take care of her. Perhaps she hasn't made much of an impact with her work because she's been sinking her attention into him.

The woman I am obsessed with slowly fills her newly rented or bought flat with art. She has a real Chris Ofili, a small vibrant orange painting, a colourful Charles Ray flower drawing, an early Wayne Thiebaud painting gifted to her father and then handed down to her, a John Baldessari exhibition poster from 1988, two Arthur Jafa photographs, she has a large Isamu Noguchi Akari ceiling lamp which is around $900, a tall Carmen D'Apolloino lamp which is a price on request with no contact information provided, almost as if you need to be friends with her in order to buy one. I don't know the cultural significance of the lamps. I don't know how she knows what painters to buy, how she is able to buy delicate, vulnerable paintings from such formidable figures in the art world. Her imagination is full of men. She has all of her art framed to gallery-exhibition level, no cheap plastic Etsy frames for her. The framer compliments her taste in being so bold and brave in her colour choices. I read the caption and the man I want to be with is mentioned next to her name. I swipe through and the last one is a photograph he has also given to me. She has asked the framer to put it in a pink frame. A pink, custom-made frame, it offsets the blue in the photo perfectly. So, she and the man I want to be with are talking again. The betrayal is like being stabbed. She is back in the picture. He has clearly given this photograph to her as a house-warming gift as you can't buy it anymore. The only place she could have got it was directly from him. He has told me terrible things about her, how glad he is to be rid of her and here she is framing something he has recently given to her, which he has also given to me, which she has lovingly placed in a handmade frame, which she has paid for, and she is complimented for her taste yet again. For her aesthetic. I clad mine in a plastic, mass-produced, indistinct gold frame from Etsy for twenty quid and dithered about the purchase for three days because I didn't want to spend the money, I thought it was too much for a frame. Up on my wall, I have a Steve McQueen poster that I took from a free stack from his show at Tate Modern. I look at Chris Ofili's work through a computer screen or on my phone. I love his night paintings, I saw them in New York on a terrible rainy day with my friend when she was living in Brooklyn for six months, where I turned up to stay with her for four days, with no money just enough for the flight and a tiny amount extra for food but then I lost all my cash on the first day. We were both in a bad mood but I insisted we go and it took two hours to get there on the subway. We only had forty-five minutes before the gallery closed and we spent most of it in the dimly lit room with his seductive paintings of the Trinidadian moonlight burnt into the canvas. He laid silver under the black and blue to make the bruise colours shimmer. You must be patient. They call to you in a whisper and then when your eyes are adjusted, they step forward and announce themselves. These paintings are remote and unattainable to me—they are one-offs, imbued with magic. Yet nothing is unattainable for the woman I am obsessed with. I have this memory of Chris Ofili but she opens her eyes to him every day. She is an equal to these names, or at least sees herself as equal to these names and lives with real life art that I can't afford and wouldn't know how to get and I put posters up with Blu Tack like I'm still fifteen years old. Like a fan.

tell me again

I press the man I want to be with like an ingrown hair buried in my inner thigh, I press him until it hurts. I will know when I have the truth because it will feel like that same satisfaction when I finally see the single hair erupting from the centre of my pinched skin, followed by the sudden eruption of blood. One day in the café before we go to see an Olafur Eliasson show, he tells me that he named children with her in bed. She told him the name she liked and he says he picked Sunshine because he thought it was funny because the sun is endlessly oppressive in California. I walk outside the café to take a breather because I feel like I've been winded. The teeth in my stomach shake me, this image of them,entwined, becomes my personal poltergeist. As if he suddenly punched me in the face, I start crying, a thousand tiny shards of light.

the lord's work

Every week, I dm the posts from Terroir to Diet Prada and
I say, look at this web-shop culturally appropriating these objects.

the grinch is an edgelord

The man I want to be with could be my sugar daddy, I could be paid but he resists this too because an outright sugar baby situation doesn't suit him either, it is too bald in its reality, there's not enough illusion there and you would have too much agency. He wants to experience your love from you, experience your hope and longing for him, he wants to experience your crazed searching for him and he wants to experience his hiding, but the decision of it, even the transactional nature of it, has to be on his side, it does not reside with you. You will not be the one to make the decisions about the two of you. He will delay and say, give me a month to think about it, give me two, which as an avoidance tactic works for a while and then you realise, this is it, there is no place to move forward. There is not much beyond the small amounts he can give. He places a building block down with you but elsewhere on his own, he will break one, two, three, so there is a stasis or regression in the work.

Although he has a profound empathy for the hungry, for immigrants, for those wronged and having suffered injustice and has a respect for people with fringe passions and beliefs who might be scorned by regular society, this does not extend to you asking to be loved. By the fact of your gender, you are fundamentally dismissed and because you are asking for his vulnerability, you become the enemy, you are treated as a hostile invader, with suspicion, surveyed as a constant high-level threat and you will be suppressed or defeated. You are judged by him as lesser for loving him. He projects his self-loathing on to you and you carry it thinking if you skim off the scum maybe something good will come eventually. He enforces an authoritarian top-down system, there is no collaboration, you will have no voice or power. When he is confronted, there is only his gaping silence and your pain. Your protests will never amount to real change, only promises there might be and then lapse back into the status quo which only serves him. He reasons, he is betraying no one if he hasn't given himself over fully to anyone and so there is no story he builds with you. It is moments only and they lead nowhere and to nothing.

The man I want to be with's behaviour is indulged by his fans. He is held aloft and alight both inside and outside of his industry. He has unfettered access to almost anyone he wants. The people he is kindest to are the ones who do not know him. The love he receives from his base gets him used to things being one-sided, he never has to work at anything, never has to work on his insides because so much is projected onto him.

There is an easy kind of love and it is fanatical adulation. Fans take their heroes and make them a part of their identity and so it becomes unbearable to ever really take in rumours of bad behaviour. We want them to remain perfect in order that we can telegraph or offload certain archetypes on to them: the truth teller, the champion, the maverick, the trickster. If we turn people into symbols and then create a fandom around them, we don't have to take on those responsibilities ourselves. They become our spokesperson nominated to do this for us so we can carry on living our lives unperturbed. These people are only human and when they commit acts of harm, we hold knowing and not knowing together, it is called an 'open secret'. Silence is tacitly demanded from gatekeepers and fevered fans. The small voices oblige. We demand this suppression. We see the small voices' sacrifice as a justified one, serving a greater cause, which is the ability to love our idol. Every single person is implicated when a small voice is hurt by a person we pedestalled and totemised. Every single fan.

genie

To entice me into bed in such a way that I beg for it, the man I want to be with tells me he has witnessed very intense orgasms from the women he has slept with. He tells me this in such a way to seduce me and says, I can make you have visions. When he fucks me the third time, which is the first time I enjoy it, I do have a vision. While I am on top of him in a first-floor hotel room in Kings Cross, I have a vision of being alone, underwater, surrounded by black and blue knotted nets.

stop teaching men words

The man I want to be with's work centres around conflict and when he is levelled with a question around the lack of women evident in his career, he says the nature of conflict is that it is about war and war has traditionally been fought by men against men. He has a clever answer for everything and now frames his work as questioning patriarchal power. He has more recently been on panels with women and been the only man—I have no idea what makes him qualified to be the only man on these panels. I erupt with rage and at nothing other than my phone when I see his concerned face in response to their opinions, his making space for them to talk, deferring to their experience and downplaying his own. I think what would these activist women think of him if they really knew him. These women who want to fight patriarchal systems, who ask questions of each other like, what would a more horizontal society look like—more female, non-binary or trans-led—and he nods respectfully making notes as they talk and answering their specific points. I am seething. My experience of him is as deadening as a border wall, he refuses to give me any specific answers to my questions and keeps me hanging in limbo. I watch him dreaming of utopian futures with these women he doesn't know but keeps me in a kind of purgatory where he forgets what he said to me a year ago, two weeks ago, sometimes saying he wants children with me and then forgetting it a minute later asking me with puzzlement at what I'm talking about. I think I am losing my mind because I am so desperate to have him and I cannot shift us from this revving first gear. I think about what he's done to all of us, what would these women on these panels say if I sent them screenshots of the emails he sends me where he admits he has a seam of misogyny running inside him and that yes, he doesn't trust women, he doesn't want to be vulnerable, he's afraid of us and wants us at the same time so he treats us badly, that for this reason I should get away from him but he needs me and isn't himself without me. What would they say to that?

love that for you

He takes me to Koya. As we sit down the man I want to be with tells me it's his favourite restaurant. I don't know how to use chopsticks and he says, you know everything how can you not know how to use chopsticks. He wants to take me to St. John in Farringdon. He tells me he knows a place and takes me to Paul Rothe & Son and we open the door to a time travel portal where the dial hasn't moved since the thirties, where the English would stop to get toast and tea at eleven in the morning. I order a cheese sandwich on white bread and a cup of sweet tea and when the waiter puts it down he says, who has the child's palette and I say, me. The man I want to be with asks me if I know these places and I say no, except I do know them, they are the woman I am obsessed with's favourite restaurants too. When I eat my cheese sandwich, I want to ask him if he brought her here or if she brought him here and how is it possible they have the same favourite restaurants if they haven't been to these places together.

I can absolutely feel as if it were inside my own body, how excruciatingly happy the woman I am obsessed with is from her Instagram. She is busy homemaking, posting photos of her geranium houseplants in the Marfa light, views from her windows exclaiming how near she is to The Chinati Foundation, comparing the landscape to the Accona desert in Tuscany, asking her community if they know any framers who specialise in 'high end' or 'custom framers' of posters, of her matching Arne Wahl Iversen teak lounge chairs (about $1500 each from what I can guess), her matching Cesca dining chairs, her nineteenth-century Zapotec rugs and her antique face jugs. She is buzzing with a kind of maddening ecstasy that is almost too much to bear. It feels high-pitched and overwhelming. It is very annoying how happy she is at the moment. Then I am reminded of how old she is and how single she is, how much she wants children and how far away that is right now for her, and I draw some comfort from that.

Things are truly bad when, at the park, a dog bounds over to where the man I want to be with and I are sitting and he pets and coos over the dog so warmly and indulgently and I sit there un-petted and un-cooed over and I start to feel jealous about the way he is with this animal because he is not this way with me. That's really when you should be thinking about getting out. When you start getting jealous of a dog.

I nod because I think this is the best thing to do and say little because it is also the best thing to do. Djuna is in a different financial bracket to me, but I can be a good listener, that's my special trick. I can reflect people back at them and I will do this to her, make it all about her and she will think I am so nice. She can fill me up with what she needs me to be. An impartial listener who is not part of her life but that's the benefit, I don't know anyone she's talking about—at least not physically. I know what their shit will look like by virtue of their documenting every fucking morsel of what is put into their bodies but they don't know my name. Milo and Mocha are playing in front of us. They are fast friends now. Mocha recognises her and Milo brings him flowers to sniff. It's very sweet. We sit on what's become our park bench and we talk. What starts as a small, ten-minute conversation gradually becomes longer and longer and we soon come to something approximating friends. I reveal little of my life except to say I am going through a break-up which explains why I'm quiet or else why I don't have much to say about myself because who the fuck goes out when they're depressed and heartbroken but I try not to be a downer. I make sure I have glowing skin and clean, pressed clothes in black, white and deep blue. She talks about Milo, about her husband and their marriage, which seems stable and full of love though she misses her childhood spent in St Ives. She mentions the woman I am obsessed with a couple of times, talks about how wonderful she is, how funny, how she secretly feels sorry for her, about her bad luck in relationships but that she's such a special, gifted person she'll find someone someday. She tells me there was someone, someone notable who she was with that fucked her life up and she's suffered ever since. I feign disinterest but the teeth in my stomach start chomping at the bit for more. While we watch Milo and Mocha playing in the grass, Djuna says she's told her sister that she's made a new friend at the park.

girls be like are you sure are you sure
are you sure are you sure are you sure

In writing countless emails and letters to the man I want to be with, I rack up hundreds of hours of writing practice. He is the first person I believe when he tells me I should do nothing but write. I would gift him books when we met for sex—I gave him Orwell, Nelson, Ishiguro and Tanizaki but because I wrote little messages in them, he has hidden them in his flat and never read them for fear of being found out.

for the plot

The man I want to be with tells me he's going to be in Glasgow with some friends of his. The day he leaves he emails me a goodbye and I reply, it was going to be a surprise but I'm jumping on a flight in a couple of hours, I'm going to be joining you! don't worry about missing me, I'll just wait in the town centre and you can come and pick me up. He emails back, I can't see you I don't know when I'll be able to get out of my thing, I'm not sure this is such a great idea. I say, don't worry I'll wait for you, you come get me when you're ready, and he emails back within the minute and says, I really don't think I can, I won't be able to see you. I wait ten minutes to give him enough time to have a panic attack about it and then email back, relax, I was just pulling your leg, as if I'd turn up in Scotland like a beg. He emails back, fuck, you had me, and I reply, did you really think I would, he writes, I wouldn't put it past you to do something like this.

The man I want to be with invites me to an event with him. He tells me he'd like me to be there. I say no because there will be a lot of fervent fans of his and I don't want to entertain the chance of being ignored or treated as part of the crowd because he will pick and choose the way he wants me to be associated with him, oscillating between girlfriend or friend or nothing. I want to see what he does when he thinks I'm not going to be there. On the day of the event, I put on a blue-black slip dress, a House of Sunny cardigan, no bra, Doc Martins and a lot of eyeliner on my top lid the way he likes it. I don't wear any perfume because he likes the smell of me, he always takes a surreptitious sniff of my neck and the top of my head when we are close together and without fail says no one smells like you and I'm immediately wet. The event is in Tottenham, close to the Overground station in a derelict looking warehouse. When I get there, there are a lot of people streaming in. I don't see the man I want to be with, he must be inside. My hand is stamped and I go down the stairs to a bare room with a screen set up and primary school chairs laid out. I take a seat at the back. It's very busy and there is a crowd around someone who I assume is the man I want to be with. I try to catch his eye but he's engrossed in conversation with someone and then he turns his back. I look around the room to see if there's anyone else I know. I get my phone out to text him to tell him, I am at the back of the room, surprise! when I see his wife exit the loo and take a seat in the middle, turning occasionally to speak to her friend who is sat beside her. I didn't expect her to be here. My blood freezes and I sense it going into reverse, my face is very hot. Finally, I get to see her in the flesh. I absorb her body. It is a record of the care she's expended on him. She wasn't a knockout when she was younger but she didn't look like this, her features have spread thickly across her face. As I stare at the back of her head, the man I want to be with turns and looks straight at me, his eyes bulge out and he turns away again. There are waves of people waiting to speak to him. I text him, shit I didn't think you'd be here with her. He texts back, I thought you weren't coming. I think about the time I was at an anti-Brexit march and he was there and I walked about trying to find him frustrated he wouldn't tell me where he was and then he said he was there with his wife and their friends, if he'd known I was going to be there he would have come on his own. He ignores me for the evening. He and his wife don't appear to be together either. She stays with her friend and she and the man I want to be with don't mingle together or hold one another when they talk to people, the way he was with me that one time we went out. When the event is over, people want to take photos of him and with him but I leave at the earliest possible opportunity, ducking my head, saying nothing as I leave the room.

rhythm o marina abramović

Seventy-two objects associated with pain or pleasure are laid out on a table. Amongst them are a rose, a feather, grapes, lipstick, honey, a whip, a scalpel, a gun and a bullet. Abramović stands in the centre of the room for six hours and surrenders herself to the audience. At the beginning the audience are timid and nervous. They reposition Abramović's arms and tentatively engage with her. As the performance matures, they are bolder. They place objects on her, take pictures of her and pose with her, taking staged photographs playing with her body, using it as a prop. They become comfortable with her inertness which makes them aggressive, pouring oil on her head, pricking her with the thorns of the rose, they cut her clothing, cut her body, they place the knife between her legs driving the blade into the wood behind her, they carry her around the room half-naked, one participant licks her blood and another loads the bullet in the gun and points it at her head and holds it there, finger on the trigger until another audience member pushes his hand away. When the gallerist announces the end of the performance, Abramović comes alive and walks about the space of her own agency. The audience members scatter, unable to bear or deal with the reminder that she is, in fact, a person. She says of the performance, it was six hours of horror and if you leave it up to the audience, they can kill you.

sign it and see

His wife doesn't exist as a protagonist on any platform, not even on Facebook. There are only old photos and obscure mentions of her through other people on Instagram. It's as if she thinks she's better than the rest of us, her ability to protect her privacy and to abstain from the internet and our collective narcissism. I follow her scant hashtag and it is how I find out she has a show and quite a big one. I call the man I want to be with and ask him if he thinks her work is good and he says it is. I flare. The teeth in my stomach flash and I lurch. I ask if he pulled any strings to get her in and he says, she is there on her own merit, but I suspect this to be false, he and the curator are good friends.

I decide to visit the gallery a week after the show opens and I decide to go alone. The gallery is vast and concrete. I've chosen a grey, rainy day, no one will come into town so I can have the space to myself. I take a map from the front door which guides me to where her name has been pinned to the white wall. When I reach her collages, there are already two people absent-mindedly looking at them in front of me. I watch the first one glaze over as he swings his body past them, looking for the next thing, for something else to catch his eye. I watch the other tilt her head trying to figure out if she feels something, then realise, no she doesn't feel anything. When they move, and I have her work to myself, I stand before them, shaking with envy and fear. It is like she is finally speaking to me and I am able to see what could happen to my insides if I gave myself away to him. Her palette is black, mauve, washed-out blues and greys, like having an old colour television on—the less vibrant options are the ones she chooses. She combines photographs with paint and presents amorphous, lonely, disembodied figures from the back so there is no emotion to connect to, no context around them, the imagery sits on the surface avoids pulling you in or under. I am reassured when I look at them but I am desperately sad. I look to the labels on the walls. Dry and rasping one-word titles and her name. Of all the words in the English language these are the ones she chooses, it feels momentous, like hearing a child's first words. The writer tasked with the description of her work seems to lose enthusiasm halfway through but perhaps this is my projection. I notice, everyone else's work in the show belongs to other people, has had to be loaned or shipped in but her work belongs to her, 'courtesy of the artist', a glaring declaration no one else wants her. I stand there so long I am afraid I look suspicious. The attendant walks away for his break before someone new covers his spot. I am alone. I take a black Sharpie out of my bag and carve my initials into the black. Below it I write, fuck you, and I walk away. When I exit the gallery, the security guard holds the door open and I smile.

gee's bend quiltmakers, alison jacques gallery

The various menstrual stains on the Gee's Bend quilts are a wonderfully bracing announcement of the body in what are usually sterile white cube gallery environments. These rust-coloured blood stains are familiar to anyone who experiences periods, where you might leak onto the bedding in the night or are the manifestation of the constant anxiety of sitting on top of material hoping you do not leave a trace of yourself on the fabric of the furniture with your blood. The bold declaration of this, free of shame, signposted nowhere in the text, on the website, or in the gallery is interesting—why not mention it? Or is the not needing to mention it the more radical thing? Or did they not notice? These quilts are made by generation upon generation of African American women from a bend in the Alabama River in a hamlet called Boykin—locally referred to as the Gee's Bend and some of the makers there, like Mary Lee Bendolph have since become renowned. The community who live in Boykin are almost all descendants of the slaves who worked on the nearby Pettway plantation and many still bear this name. The quilts are seen as an important chapter of American art combining historical pattern-making with geometric design. What is all the more poetic is that they were not made for display or for the market but to be used by the family. The women of Boykin would collect scraps of material and stitch them together to insulate their children's beds. Every spring there is a community airing out of the quilts where on the lines, the women will inspect, borrow techniques, compete and be inspired by each other's quilts for the next year. This making something useful and whole and healing out of fragments of fabric, out of what is left over and unwanted speaks to so much more than keeping warm.

The woman I am obsessed with causes me untold turbulence and outrage but for her fans and friends she is a grounding and calming presence. She has a particularly grating voice but is told it is soothing like honey, able to magic away tension and stress in all who hear her. To me her voice rings nasally, she has a languid vocal fry which infuses her words. She uses archaic words, or else long words to describe simple things, like *lacustrine*, *pellucid*, *provenance*, which shows the pedigree of her education but also her total detachment from real life. Her written voice is stilted, overworked, overwritten and gives me this strange buzzing feeling and I can't make sense of what she is saying. She thinks she is really funny but she just laughs loudly to herself at her own 'jokes'. What everyone admires her for is buying things well, which isn't so much a skill but then maybe it is because I cannot do it. When I first looked at her profile and I saw the blue tick, the tens of thousands of followers, my hands shook. Why does the man I want to be with want anything to do with me when this woman has everything? Anything she says is given extra heft because of this blue tick, she is given privileges from the machine and then is also gifted more because of the tick, receives grateful thanks from whatever business owner she highlights in her posts or stories. I post the story of the Gee's Bend quilts and get a private like for my story in the dms from the gallery, but if the woman I am obsessed with did the same, her followers and her blue tick would have got her much more attention, so much more gratitude. She was bequeathed this tick because of the luck and randomness of genetics, because of the life she was born into and the benefits and access she is given, which led to an aspirational life which she posts on the machine, is given this blue tick by the machine and then because of this blue tick, is further enhanced by the machine—I don't think her publisher would have dropped such a huge advance without it. She has a head start and is given additional benefits so runs forever out of my league. The endless replication of her whiteness on Instagram was given a wake-up call in the summer of 2020. She now posts stories of tweets from prominent Black activists or else, at the time of Derek Chauvin's trial, reposts stories of tweets from Black people where they say, do not celebrate this verdict, there is so much more work to do—as if she too is so evolved and in step with the conversation. Liberal whites have got much better at disguising themselves post George Floyd—now they will post photos from their Thanksgiving dinner and say, holding what this day means *and* the joy at being with friends.

The woman I am obsessed with says she is sad and worried about the state of America and I think, it's a funny thing to feel sad— or feel anything about racism because what a luxury. She is able to disregard that America has always been a white European genocidal project, a settler-colonial state founded upon death and violence. It has never demonstrated the soaring values the American founders myth insists upon. Believing this falsified story, saying, *we are capable of more, this isn't us* rather than that bone-tired weariness of, *we always said it was this, we always told you but you didn't believe us when it happened to us but you believe it now it is happening to you*—is Exceptionalism. It is the same brand which is pushed by populist leaders and has the same tang of denial where the country and its people cannot collectively reckon with its racist and colonial past. Her feeling sad about what happens when an unfair verdict is passed or yet another Black person is murdered at the hands of vigilantes or the police means she expects more from a country and its systems, which have always suppressed and dehumanised the Indigenous population it removed and the Black people it brought over in order to make a profit. She doesn't understand what racism really is. She only posts the exceptional things Black people do on her grid.

job

The woman I am obsessed with reposts a story from a friend she grew up with who has opened a similar failing-to-make-a-profit interiors business and is advertising for a part-time worker. I could apply. I could wear my Ganni tracksuit or else something large and flowing with big sleeves. I want to look expensive and careless like they do, I could apply and get it, and say whatever it is I needed to say. I would work from her friend's home, I would apply make-up every day and I would wait for her to come round, I would be quiet at first and ignore her and I would pretend not to know who she is, I could seduce her with flowers on the table, a scented candle burning on my desk, I could offer to make them my mother's food or make her one of her own recipes and when she says, this is how I make that, I could say, oh my family have been making it like this for years and I would feel familiar to her. I want to feel familiar to her.

new clothes

Women are beautiful, alluring but terrifying forces and the way to deal with terrifying forces is to break them. The man I want to be with's desire for me, or any woman, is experienced as an unbearable oppression. He is at the top of society in so many ways, being subservient to his sexual desire is the closest thing he has to feeling powerless. He cannot bear a woman to have control over him and sees our sexuality as a threat, set out purposefully to destroy him which he must evade at all costs. In his failure to experience and take responsibility for his own sexuality, he seeks to nuke the woman yet simultaneously casts himself as the victim so the woman he is destroying still takes care of him as she is brought down. You collaborate in your own destruction. He tells me he is scared of emotional intimacy and he is the worst to the people who love him the most. He's aware of it all but doesn't want to change any of it. If he changed any of it, it would have implications for his working life and he doesn't want to risk it. He would rather protect his death drive. His love is expressed as hatred and contempt though it has a face of wonder. It is heterosexuality as misogynistic fascist fervour. Men have all this power and this is the world they have created, where everyone experiences only slivers of snatched joy. There is no space for expansive and evolving creativity, only insecurity and homogeny are fostered where straight men uphold one another through a homoerotic bond, or are complicit through silence. No matter how much some say they respect women, each man, even the 'good ones', benefit from women's low expectations of them as control is exerted via a climate of instability, fear and violence.

The man I want to be with wants you most when you do not

want him, he prefers the chase. The point at which you become emotionally invested is the exact moment he loses interest. This is met with my own wounding where I want what doesn't want me. He wants the consistency from a mother and not the conditionality of a lover. When I pointlessly argue and fight with him, I feel like I am fighting the very structures of the old colonial forces, where he has, holds and takes, and I give, offer and ask for nothing in return. We all have teeth in our stomach for him. We are all sacrificed at the altar of his fear.

custard

Around me everyone is booking holidays, buying houses, moving in together, moving out together, celebrating their wins for one another, holding their babies. They rush back home after work to see their loved ones, say *yeah yeah see you tomorrow* as they are out of the door to see the people they have chosen, who have chosen them. There is sweetness all around me and I am a hard bitter fig. Everyone I know seems to move quite easily into acquiring the symbols of adulthood. My friends tell me they have shifting priorities for our friendship, perhaps we are not so aligned any more, they can't be as available as they were when we were younger. They have responsibilities now.

The woman I am obsessed with is screeching with happiness in her new home. She posts thirty stories up like she did back in the old days plotting her every movement except this time she doesn't put up the faces of the people she is with, instead she posts empty dressed tables before her dinner parties or abstracted close-ups of the food. Her followers climb up by the hundreds, which pushes the total figure further into the thousands. Her followers congratulate her when she is back home, welcome her to whatever new city she ordains, fall over themselves to recommend places they know she should eat at or visit, are very concerned if she has a good time or not. They write down personal memories—almost essays—in her comments if she goes somewhere they have a connection to in order to be closer to her. Maybe she will write back to them and interact with them in some way. Her post count racks up from two thousand to three thousand.

The man I want to be with's Twitter hashtag is updated and I see he has a talk in the countryside, a famous literary house has invited him to talk about something no one gives a shit about anymore. A friend of his wife's has a painting show in the gallery of this literary house and I suspect she will go with him. On the day of the talk, I refresh both his Twitter and his Instagram hashtag and there is nothing. The next morning, I check again and one of his friends has posted a picture of the man I want to be with and his wife framed by a hysterical burst of intensely coloured hollyhocks, the sunlight flaring off the corners of a cottage in the background. Though they aren't holding hands, they touch at the shoulder and the elbow and the wrist. He is somehow neutered next to her, less of a man, more like a child. He looks like her old son. She is grinning straight into the lens and he looks off camera with an enigmatic smile on his face. It could be happiness or safety but aren't they the same thing. If I loved them, I would say it was a beautiful photograph.

The man I want to be with sends me an email. In it he says he'd like us to take a break in communication. He says he could live more days like the ones we share but I'm right, he does need to make up his mind about me but he's unable to think about us as I am so available to him so maybe we shouldn't talk. I don't reply. Two months pass. I break and text him, thinking surely things will turn around now, he has suffered enough. He replies straightaway, as if he's had his phone in his hand the entire time we haven't been speaking, waiting for me to reach out to him and says he's been thinking about me, I ask how and he says, good things, your energy, how you are, sex. My eyebrows shoot up at the last word. It has been three years since he let us sleep together. He says, maybe we should have sex or is that a terrible idea? I say, it would be nice but it's probably a bad idea, he says, ok I understand, without you it is more boring but more restful, I don't move but I do miss you and maybe if we just had sex it would be ok or probably not! I could say, yes, actually, fuck it why not, I could say, yes let's sleep together, he'd book a hotel the way we did a few years ago, we'd get in the room, he would have a shower first and then I'd take my clothes off. We'd had unprotected sex before—I wasn't on the pill and he didn't ask and I didn't say. I made him pull out and come in my mouth but this time I could ride him and force him to stay inside me when he comes, I could say, I'm on the pill it's ok, or maybe he wouldn't ask, my cunt shrouded in a secret we would enjoy together. There is something so transgressive and reckless about the idea of having a man come inside me, refusing the science available to prevent the inevitable, a rebellion against the separateness we insist upon, the throbbing of his penis shooting all his semen inside me, of our bodies doing what they want to do with no interference from machine logic, there is a sick thrill in conjoining all our ancient animal parts and knowingly ruining my life and doing it with reckless abandon. He would ask, did you come, and I would say, no, because I have never come with him, I never felt safe enough to. Instead I would clench to keep his sperm incubated inside my body. I would throw myself flat down on the bed, raise my legs up, rock side to side like I've seen women do on television. I could curl up like a scorpion, hold him hostage, a piece of him all mine—

Acknowledgements

To my family, especially my mother. To Victoria Smart for being my first reader. Thank you to Olivia Sudjic and Niven Govinden for being such top tier early readers. To BK for your support and your love. Thank you to my agent Lucy Luck for your magic. To Craig Oldham for making the hardback edition a sexy stunner. To Kate McQuaid and Susanna Grant for being protectors. To LD, thank you for your everlasting cocoon. To Jason Arthur and the Granta team, thank you for a beautiful edition and for letting me join your literary family. To my sister poets, Roshni Goyate, Sharan Hunjan & Sunnah Khan without whom I wouldn't be writing, I carry you with me always and you are here in the pages of this book. And finally, the deepest gratitude to Nina Hervé for asking the question and to Will Burns for answering it, I love you both so much x